# INFANT HOLY, INFANT LOWLY

Advent Family Worship
with the
Carols of Christmas

# INFANT HOLY, INFANT LOWLY

Advent Family Worship
with the
Carols of Christmas

DOUGLAS BOND

SCRIPTORIUM
PRESS

Also, by Douglas Bond

*Mr. Pipes and the British Hymn Makers*
*Mr. Pipes and Psalms and Hymns of the Reformation*
*Mr. Pipes Comes to America*
*The Accidental Voyage*

*Duncan's War*
*King's Arrow*
*Rebel's Keep*

*Guns of Thunder*
*Guns of the Lion*
*Guns of Providence*

*Hostage Lands*
*Hand of Vengeance*
*Hammer of the Huguenots*
*The Battle of Seattle*
*War in the Wasteland*
*The Resistance*
*The Hobgoblins*

*STAND FAST In the Way of Truth*
*HOLD FAST In a Broken World*

*The Betrayal: A Novel on John Calvin*
*The Thunder: A Novel on John Knox*
*The Revolt: A Novel in Wycliffe's England*
*Luther in Love*

*The Mighty Weakness of John Knox*
*The Poetic Wonder of Isaac Watts*

*Augustus Toplady: Debtor to Mercy Alone*
*Girolamo Savonarola: Heart Aflame*

*Grace Works! (And Ways We Think It Doesn't)*
*God Sings! (And Ways We Think He Ought To)*

*God's Servant Job*
*God's Servant Ruth*

*EVANGELICAL HEROES*
*(Vols 1 & 2, with Joel Beeke)*

ISBN: 978-1-945062-21-6 (pbk.)
ISBN: 978-1-945062-22-3 (ePub)

Cover designed by Robert Treskillard.

Cover art: Cantoria, Luca della Robbia (1431-1438)

Printed in the United States of America

Library of Congress Cataloging-in-Publication Data

Bond, Douglas, 1958-

Infant Holy, Infant Lowly / Douglas Bond. – 1st [edition].

pages cm

Summary: Advent family devotionals based on the carols, their biblical sources, their poets, and composers; for reading, discussing, and singing together from November 30 to December 25.

ISBN: 978-1-945062-21-6 (pbk.)

1. Family and relationships—parenting/fatherhood. 2. Music—religious/Christian. 3. Religion/Christian rituals and practice/worship and liturgy. I. Title.

BT761.3.B66 2025
234--dc23

2025049333

I cherish my childhood memories
of family worship,
and offer this little volume
with deepest gratitude and
in memory of my beloved parents,
Douglas Elwood Bond (1933-2006)
and Mary Jane Bond (1937-2025)

I also cherish my memories as a father
leading my six children in family worship.
I commend the Object of this book,
Jesus the Messiah of Advent,
to my children and my grandchildren

and to Christian families everywhere

"Christ is still in Christmas, and for one brief season the secular world broadcasts the message of Christ over every radio station and television channel in the land. Never does the church get as much free air time as during the Christmas season."

R. C. Sproul

"Next to the Word of God, music deserves the highest praise. … But any who remain unaffected [by music] are clodhoppers indeed and are fit to hear only the words of dung-poets and the music of pigs."

Martin Luther

"The purpose of theology is doxology… Any theology that does not lead to song is, at a fundamental level, a flawed theology."

J. I. Packer

"'It's Christmas!' I was ready to walk right through that door into heaven."

R. C. Sproul (his first Christmas as a Christian)

# CONTENTS

**Come, Thou Long Expected Jesus**

Charles Wesley (1707-1742)

Advent Eve Preface

(November 30)

Come, thou long expected Jesus,
Born to set thy people free;
From our fears and sins release us,
Let us find our rest in thee.
Israel's strength and consolation,
Hope of all the earth thou art;
Dear desire of every nation,
Joy of every longing heart.

Born thy people to deliver,
Born a child and yet a King,

Born to reign in us forever,
Now thy gracious kingdom bring.

By thine own eternal spirit
Rule in all our hearts alone;
By thine all-sufficient merit,
Raise us to thy glorious throne.

Have you ever wondered what makes Christmas such an enchanting time of year? We love the lights, the decorations, the garlands and trees, the nutcrackers, the sleigh bells, and all those Christmas cookies and candy! But can you imagine all these without music?

**Music and Christmas**

Christmas music has a great deal to do with the wonder of Advent, Jesus' first coming; we hear it in the car, and on our devices; we hear it while shopping for gifts, and we sing Christmas carols at church. But what is it that makes a particular kind of song a carol, a song uniquely appropriate to be sung at Christmas? In these daily Advent family devotions, we will explore the best Christmas carols, their authors, the music to which they are set, and discover what makes these hymns about Advent so special to us.

Like a beautiful tapestry, both the lyric (the words) and the music of the finest carols are interlaced, are expertly woven together. They awaken something deep within us, something marvelous beyond words, something that transports us from our everyday, ordinary lives, into celestial splendors, too high to grasp, too deep for words.

And yet we are singing words! We are hearing music! Conjoining together, those words and music transport us into the immeasurable vault of eternal things, things too high and beautiful for mere words. Which is part of the reason God made us to make poetry and music! And a particular kind of music, music to sing at Advent, the culmination of millennia (thousands of years) of prophesies, the pinnacle about which all redemptive history has been directing our undivided attention.

And here we are at Advent, once again. Our pulse quickens. We laugh more easily. We feel the rustle of anticipation. Something is coming, something wonderful!

**Advent and joy**

Whatever woes press down upon our lives, whatever affliction, whatever suffering, whatever illness, whatever sadness, whatever grief, whatever loss and loneliness—we long for Advent, for the coming, for the promised Messiah, the Anointed One, the one who alone heals all of our diseases, makes right every wrong, restores every shattered thing, brings us near to God, bears our griefs, our sorrows, and ultimately bears all of our sins in his own body.

In order for there to be such inexpressible joy, joy that cannot be measured or contained, there must first be sorrow, there must be loss, there must be emptiness. Only the lost can be saved. Light only shines clear that dispels darkness. Something about Advent, something about Christmas, awakens the light, rouses us to truth and beauty inexpressible. And yet we feel compelled to express it! And what better way than in carols—timeless, enduring lyrics, composed throughout the ages, set to music that makes not only our voices, but our hearts to sing.

We are tempted to think that it is just the crackling fire and warmth around the hearth while it's cold outside, that makes for this stupendous season, the feelings and longings that we have during such a season. We are tempted to think it is the twinkling lights, the special sweets, Grandma's homemade Almond Roca, the good cheer, the ribbons and gifts, the decorations on the tree, the reuniting of families, the easy laughter, the hugs—the cold outside and the glowing warmth inside.

But it must be something much greater than these things. At the end of the evening, at the end of the season when we take all the glittering decorations down, put the tree on the curb to be picked up by garbage collectors, stuff all that beauty away and stow the ornaments in boxes in the attic. There has to be something more. It can't be just sentimental warm fuzzies, a season of good cheer we invent to hold off the frigid winter weather, and the emptiness inside each one of us. And then it's over.

**What's so special about Christmas?**

But what is it? It's none of these things in and of themselves. It's not a thing at all. It's a Person. It's the coming of the baby in the manger, the "Joy of every longing heart."

Who doesn't love babies? But this was no ordinary baby. This infant was like no other. The baby born to Mary in a cattle stall was unique. For millennia, the ancient prophets had foretold that uniqueness, "Israel's strength and consolation." This baby was the Son of God, "Born a child and yet a King."

Irony of ironies, the Creator of the universe had stooped to become a creature, but not any creature; an infant, a baby for whom his parents had to do everything; a baby born to the working poor, a fourteen-year-old virgin mother and a bewildered carpenter father, the most common of people from a nowheresville, backwater town—but an infant who would be the High Priest and the ultimate sacrifice, the Lamb of God who came for one purpose: to fulfill all righteousness and die for the sins of his people. And then to "Rule in all our hearts alone."

No wonder we sing at Christmas. How could we be silent? No wonder we sing the most grand, transcendent lyric poetry, set to some of the most heavenly music human beings can compose. There is no greater use of poetic lines or musical notes than this. The cosmic lens is focused on this one event, on this one Person, this infant and his thirty-three years of life, ordained from all eternity, the life of Jesus, the Savior of the world. We must sing. If we do not, the very stones will shout his splendor, will sing his praises, will hail him with hosannahs. We must sing!

Jesus was born into a family, a father, a mother, later brothers, sisters. Maybe a family like yours. There's no greater context in which to sing than in families, our immediate families—fathers, mothers, siblings—and our celestial family, the church and Kingdom of Christ.

What do we sing about? A child born in Bethlehem, the "long expected Jesus," born to fulfill all righteousness, born to suffer and to die, not for his transgressions, but for ours! Born to rise again, victorious over death and hell and the devil. Born to crush the serpent's head, born to set his people free, born to give us eternal life. We must sing, sing with full voices, hearts aflame; overflowing with wonder, love, and praise for such a glorious Redeemer, Jesus born of Mary, born in Bethlehem, "Born to set [his] people free!"

**For discussion**

1. What are your favorite things about Christmas?
2. Discuss together as a family how the best Christmas carols are different from some of the silly jingles sung about Santa Claus and reindeer?
3. Christmas is many people's favorite time of year, even ones who claim not to be Christians, yet, on some level, they celebrate Christmas anyway, some even singing carols of which they don't believe a word. What do your unbelieving neighbors leave out of their celebration of Christmas?
4. Some Christmas carols are based on Old Testament prophesies of Jesus' birth. Read and discuss these prophesies written 750 years before Jesus' birth. Isaiah 7:4 and Micah 5:2.
5. What are some ways you as a family can share the true meaning of Advent, the coming of Jesus "to save his people from their sins," with your neighbors?
6. It's time to sing a Christmas carol together as a family! "Come, Thou Long Expected Jesus," was written by Charles Wesley (more about him later) and set to *Hyfrydol*, a sturdy Welsh tune by Rowland Hugh Prichard. Visit bondbooks.net/hymns to find links to the music.

**Infant Holy, Infant Lowly**

Anonymous Polish, translated and versified by
Edith Margaret Gellibrand Reed (1885-1933)
(December 1)

Infant holy,
Infant lowly,
For his bed a cattle stall;
Oxen lowing,
Little knowing
Christ the babe is Lord of all.
Swift are winging,
Angels singing,
Noels ringing,
Tidings bringing:
Christ the babe is Lord of all.
Christ the babe is Lord of all.

Flocks were sleeping,
Shepherds keeping

Vigil till the morning new
Saw the glory,
Heard the story,
Tidings of a gospel true.
Thus rejoicing,
Free from sorrow,
Praises voicing,
Greet the morrow:
Christ the Babe was born for you.
Christ the Babe was born for you.

"Infant Holy, Infant Lowly," is one of my all-time favorite carols. At family worship, when it's my turn to pick the carol, I've almost always picked this beautiful Polish carol. Beautiful. Do you ever wonder what beauty actually is? "That is so beautiful," we say about a sunset, a painting, a Medieval church building, a bouquet of flowers, a new dress, a bride at a wedding. But what do we really mean by beauty?

**What makes a carol beautiful?**

We live in a world that has attempted to make everything relative, subjective, that is to say, there are no objective standards of reality, truth, goodness, or even beauty. Everything is up for individual preferences and tastes. The primary way people think in our culture (called someone's world view) insists that there is no absolute truth, no objective reality, and no transcendent authority. Everything is just up to the individual; I decide what is true for me, what is real for me; I am my own authority; there is no authority above me. Our culture says that each individual person gets to decide what is true, what is real, and what is beautiful. There is no transcendent God, that is, a divine authority above us that reveals to us goodness, truth, and beauty. It's whatever we want it to be. There are so many problems with this world view, so much objective evidence that contradicts the belief that we could go on for a whole book about it.

Wait! There already is a whole book written about these things. The Bible! The world tells us that everything is in chaos, without any order or design. There are no foundational standards of what makes one thing beautiful and another bent and ugly. But we *do* know what beauty is—because God the Creator has revealed his beauty in creation. "The heavens declare the glory of God." The whole universe itself demonstrates what beauty is. Beauty is sometimes called "aesthetics," the study of art and what is beautiful. While the world is wearing itself out attempting to redefine what is true and what is real, it should be no surprise to Christians that the world also redefines and distorts what is beautiful.

You might be wondering what this has to do with Christmas carols. It has everything to do with them! Poetry and music are forms of aesthetics, of beauty. So, how we measure the worth and beauty of a particular poem set to music, a carol, has foundations in God's Word and in his world, in what he has revealed about what is beautiful. "Beauty is not a matter of arbitrary taste," said R. C. Sproul. Arbitrary just means random, chaotic, whatever we decide.

While the unbelieving world tries to convince itself that God's world has no underlying order or meaning or purpose, reading our Bibles, gazing with sanctified eyes at the beauty of creation all around us, we can respond to our Creator with awe and wonder, and worship and praise—and with beautiful expressions of our worship, as we do when we write or sing carols.

God's Word and world reveal that beauty has certain qualities: harmony, simplicity, complexity, and proportion. We could summarize these qualities by saying: beautiful things fit together, have depth, have richness, have mystery; and beautiful things fill us with wonder. We can see these qualities in the best carols, including "Infant Holy, Infant Lowly."

**Polish people and Christmas**

Nobody knows for sure who wrote this 13th-century Polish poem; some credit Piotr Skarga, 16th-century, devout, Jesuit Roman Catholic, staunchly intolerant of men like Martin Luther and the Protestant Reformation. Once again, we are reminded that the church sometimes meets in its hymnal. Whomever wrote this carol was clearly a devoted lover of Jesus.

Two other uniquely Polish features are important to understand. Though the Roman Catholic Church for centuries burned people at the stake for translating Scripture into the vernacular, the common language of the people, and though church services were required to be in Latin, even when the vast majority of people coming to church didn't understand a word of Latin, in Medieval Poland there was a stubborn preference for their own native Polish in church. Polish people began singing Christmas carols in their own language, who cares what the Roman Catholic bishops said! And they began singing outdoors, going from cottage to cottage in their villages, singing Polish hymns and carols to their neighbors. Does that sound familiar? Maybe Poland invented Christmas caroling!

**Translating from Polish to English**

A great deal of credit for the English poetry in this beautiful carol, however, goes to the English playwright and poet Edith M. G. Reed who stumbled across the carol and translated the Polish into English in 1920.

That's not an easy thing to do. "Poetry eludes translation," one literary professor put it. By definition, languages use different sounding words. Thus, the words that share meaning with and rhyme with the English words "lowing" and "knowing," in Polish are likely to be very different sounding. As with most hymns translated from other languages, Edith Reed used the raw material of the original Polish to create a marvelously singable English carol. We owe her a great debt for one of my favorite Christmas carols.

**Looking more closely**

Let's examine more closely how she did it. In just a few words and phrases, Edith Reed awakens our imagination and makes us feel like we were actually there, in the cattle stall where Mary laid newborn baby Jesus in a manger. This would be the "lowly" part of Jesus' birth, to be born in a barn, and laid in an animal feeding trough for his bed. The poet further shifts our point of view on the unfolding scene to the animals, to the "oxen lowing." This was an unusual event for them too! "Little knowing"! The cattle didn't fully know what was going on! Imagine if a giant ox wanted a midnight snack and leaned over to get a mouthful of hay, and there was baby Jesus smiling up at him from the feeding trough!

This simple but brilliant poetry combined with a traditional Polish melody, sounds like the mazurka dance, a type of music made popular by Polish pianist and composer Frederick Chopin.

Likely the original poet and Edith Reed knew that they were crafting poetry not for professional opera singers with vast lung capacities, but for ordinary people to sing, children and families, and for the untrained voices of the congregation of God's people to sing in church. So, they composed poetry with short rhyming lines, easier for everyone to sing.

Notice the change that takes place midway in these stanzas; something glorious begins to happen: an acceleration, a quickening of the pace, each line building with energy.

Swift are winging,
Angels singing,
Noels ringing,
Tidings bringing:

And then, when the music and the words have lifted us up to the summit of the crescendo, for an instant, there's a hovering, as we're floating, breathlessly waiting with anticipation for what follows. "Christ the babe is Lord of all," sung twice over.

The final stanza shifts from the cattle stall to the Judean hillside where "Flocks were sleeping/Shepherds keeping" (no need for a swimmer's lung capacity to sing these short lines). The sheep are suddenly awakened! So are their shepherds. Something wonderful is happening! Without warning, angels appeared above them in the night sky! Imagine the shepherds seeing the glory of the heavenly hosts, and not only hearing the story of the gospel true, but seeing it unfolding before their very eyes!

As they did in the first stanza, the poet and the composer thrill our souls midway in the second with "Tidings of a gospel true." And then, not to be outdone by the first stanza, the acceleration resumes, the quickening of the pace begins again, this time with still more vigor and expectation. Can you feel the swelling in these lines?

Thus rejoicing,
Free from sorrow,
Praises voicing,
Greet the morrow:

And then another quivering instant at the apex (like when you're jumping high on a trampoline), here on the word "morrow," followed by "Christ the babe was born for you." Wonder of wonders! Christ the babe was born for you and born for me!

Do you see it? Do you hear it? Do you feel it? The beauty of this poem and carol? It has all the qualities of true and timeless beauty (you get the idea even if you don't fully understand these words): harmony, simplicity, complexity, and proportionality. It reflects harmony, the interconnecting unity of idea and form (like when you put Legos together and they fit); it has simplicity, but not to be confused with being simplistic, something that is trite or insignificant, and lacking in substance; which leads to complexity, the comprehensive scope required to encompass the theme of the poetry (like when you try to show your mother how much you love her by spreading your arms as widely as you can reach); and Reed's carol has skillful proportionality, that is, it employs high-register language (not slang), words and phrase fitting to the grand object of the carol—the incarnation of the second person of the Triune God, the infant Jesus—who is Lord of all!

**For discussion**

1. Discuss as a family what things you all agree are beautiful (start with your mother). Is beauty just up to our personal and individual taste, what we like or don't like at any given time?
2. What are the two sources for understanding truth, reality, and beauty? Talk together as a family about how this carol has the qualities of harmony, simplicity, complexity, and proportionality.
3. Why is it a special challenge to translate poetry from one language to another?
4. What are two unique contributions made by Polish people to Christmas?
5. Read together Luke 2:8-20. Discuss the specific details about the shepherds and the angels

included in this account. What would it have been like to be there?

**Silent Night! Holy Night!**

Joseph Mohr (1792-1848)

(December 2)

Silent night! Holy night!
All is calm, all is bright
Round yon virgin mother and child!
Holy infant, so tender and mild,
Sleep in heavenly peace!
Sleep in heavenly peace!

Silent night! Holy night!
Shepherds quake at the sight!
Glories stream from heaven afar,
Heavenly hosts sing Alleluia!
Christ the Savior is born!
Christ the Savior is born!

Silent night! Holy night!

Son of God, love's pure light
Radiant beams from thy holy face
With the dawn of redeeming grace,
Jesus, Lord, at thy birth!
Jesus, Lord, at thy birth!

"Silent Night! Holy Night!" qualifies for the most world-wide popular Christmas carol of all time. Originally written in German, this carol has been translated into over 300 different languages. For all of its acclaim and popularity, it has quiet and unspectacular beginnings; there's no glamorous story about it coming into being. There is an incredible story of the carol from World War I, but the story of its beginnings is pretty ordinary—but never underestimate the ordinary!

**Writing the carol**

Austrian Roman Catholic assistant priest Joseph Mohr wrote the poem "Silent Night!" in 1816, with six original stanzas. In 1818, he suddenly got the idea to use his poem for the Christmas Eve service at his little parish church, but he had no music for it. So, he asked his friend and organist Franz Gruber to compose a melody so it could be sung as a carol for his congregation—the next night. Gruber had to hurry! Because the parish church had a chronic problem with flooding, and the organ had been damaged, Gruber composed the melody for two voices accompanied by a guitar. Only later was the tune *Stille Nacht* arranged for organ.

Gruber's hastily composed carol tune became so well-loved that it was variously credited to famous composers like Haydn, Beethoven, and Mozart! Its strength is in its pastoral simplicity, enhanced by his use of compound meter, the use of multiple notes for single syllables, as in the opening lines, Si-i-lent night! Ho-o-ly Night. Combined with the repetition beginning each stanza, the effect is one of breathless mystery and wonder at the incarnation of the Son of God—as if it were happening before our very eyes.

**Silent night on the Western Front**

"The War to End All Wars," as progressive Modernists optimistically dubbed World War I, was the most horrific war in human history up to 1914 when it began. Modern industrial war machines were the most effective at killing to date. But generals and the strategists of war continued to use old-world military strategies and tactics—ways of doing battle. Men were still sent to their certain deaths in frontal charges against the strafing firepower of machine guns, and the explosive destruction of incessant artillery fire.

Fifteen-million combatants lost their lives and another eight-million men, women, and children—non-combatants—were destroyed in the maw of the war. World-wide populations plummeted in the next two generations after the war. Many marriageable women lived out their lives as spinsters, unmarried because there simply were not enough men still alive to marry and have children and families. Too many twenty-year-old men's lives were obliterated in the war.

In defiance of international law, Germany invaded neutral Belgium on August 4, 1914. Orchestrators of the conflict on both sides were certain it would be a short war. It would be over before Christmas.

It was far from over before Christmas; five years of death and destruction lay ahead. In the European Western Front, whole armies dug into trenches to avoid being annihilated by their enemies. Hundreds of miles of trenches filled with mud, blood, and the corpses of the dead and the terrified living. It was a stalemate, a war of attrition—which army would have the most men still standing when it was over? No one knew.

Amidst the mounting casualties, on Dec. 7, 1914, Pope Benedict begged the heads of state of the embattled nations to have a Christmas truce. He asked "that the guns may fall silent at least upon the night the angels sang." The top military brass ignored his plea.

But on the night of December 24, 1914, Christmas Eve, something enchanting began rippling along hundreds of miles of battle front. It was so palpable and memorable many men wrote about it in their journals and letters home. Pvt. Albert Moren of the Second Queens Regiment described the evening, "a beautiful moonlit night, frost on the ground, white almost everywhere."

In various sectors of the front, in their misery and loneliness, men began singing. Singing Christmas carols that they had learned by heart as little boys. Graham Williams of the Fifth London Rifle Brigade wrote, "First the Germans would sing one of their carols and then we would sing one of ours... I thought, well, this is really a most extraordinary thing—two nations both singing the same carol in the middle of a war."

One war historian discovered even more specific details. A German officer named Walter Kirchhoff, who had been a soloist with the Berlin Opera before going to war, began singing. First Kirchhoff sang in his native German, "*Stille Nacht! heilige Nacht*!" his booming operatic voice carrying over the frozen carnage of no-man's-land between the opposing armies. Then he sang again, in English, "Silent night! Holy night!" The British troops joined in. German soldiers lit candles and decorated small trees and held them up on their bayonets above the trench line. Next morning, there were tense moments as men who had been intent on killing one another hours before, gradually immerged from their trenches to meet in no-man's-land, to join hands, exchange small gifts, bury their dead, sing more carols together, and even play a round of soccer.

While as many as 100,000 enemy troops spontaneously participated in the truce, and survivors of the war reminisced with wonder about the event the rest of their lives, a German corporal of the 16th Bavarians, did not approve of the fraternization. "Such a thing should not happen in wartime. Have you no German sense of honor left?" His name was Adolf Hitler.

Jesus is prophesied as the Prince of Peace (Isaiah 9:6), and the angels announced to the shepherds that the birth of Jesus would bring "peace on earth good-will toward men." Yet, since WW I there have continued to be wars and rumors of more wars. Imagine being a soldier in WW I and singing of "Jesus sleeping in heavenly peace," while all around you was the wasteland of war, a war that would grind on for years. Jesus was the Prince of Peace, but we still have wars. Think about that. In what ways did Jesus come to bring peace on earth?

**Looking more closely**

Enriched with Franz Gruber's pastoral folk melody, the poet who wrote "Silent Night!" invites us to picture three unfolding scenes. In the opening stanza, we gaze in wonder at Jesus' virgin mother giving birth to the "holy infant, so tender and mild." Jesus would be like no other man born of woman. He would never sin, never be harsh and agitated; he would be gentle and lowly; he is God. Our imaginations are awakened to think of Jesus cradled in his mother's arms, closing his eyes and going to sleep "in heavenly peace," likely surrounded by donkeys and bovine in a Bethlehem cowshed that holy night.

Next, the poet shifts the lens to the hillside outside of Bethlehem. The silent night suddenly awakened with heavenly glories filling the night sky; the terrified shepherds quaking as they heard the "heavenly hosts," real warrior angels singing, "Christ the Savior is born!"

And in the last stanza of the carol, we're guided back to gaze more closely at the face of the infant Savior, the "Son of God, love's pure light." We're invited to behold the "radiant beams from [his] holy face." At last, the Light of the world has come! Here he is! But what does it all mean? Jesus' coming was "the dawn of redeeming grace," in the sense that his birth that silent night was figuratively the dawn, the morning of something incredible.

The beginning of Jesus' earthly history would result in this holy infant growing to be a toddler, an adolescent, a teenager, an adult man—the perfectly holy man, the man of sorrows, the God-man who alone came to save his people from their sins by his "redeeming grace." That silent night, so long ago, truly was *the* holiest of nights, wherein "Christ the Savior [was] born!"

**For discussion**

1. In 1818, it was unusual to use the instrument in church that was first used to accompany this carol. What was the instrument, and why did Gruber use it?
2. What are the three scenes that make up the three stanzas of "Silent Night!"?
3. In what way could it be said that this is the most powerful carol ever sung? Give an example from 20th century history.
4. Read John 8:12 and discuss how this carol alludes to the second of Jesus' "I am" declarations.
5. Read John 18:37 and discuss together what Jesus says was his purpose for being born into this world?

**Once in Royal David's City**
Cecil Frances Alexander (1818-1895)
(December 3)

Once in royal David's city
Stood a lowly cattle shed,
Where a mother laid her baby
In a manger for his bed:
Mary was that mother mild,
Jesus Christ her little child

He came down to earth from heaven,
Who is God and Lord of all.
And his shelter was a stable,
And his cradle was a stall;
With the poor and meek and lowly,
Lived on earth our Savior holy.

And through all his wondrous childhood,
He would honor and obey,
Love and watch the lowly mother,
In whose gentle arms he lay.
Christian children all should be
Mild, obedient, good as he.

For he is our childhood's pattern;
Day by day like us he grew;
He was little, weak, and helpless,
Tears and smiles like us he knew;
And he feeleth for our sadness,
And he shareth in our gladness.

And our eyes at last shall see him
Through his own redeeming love;
For that child so dear and gentle
Is our Lord in heaven above,
And he leads his children on
To the place where he is gone.

Not in that poor lowly stable,
With the oxen standing by,
We shall see him, but in heaven,
Set at God's right hand on high;
When like stars his children crowned,
All in white shall wait around.

**A carol for children**

Deeply devoted to the Christian education of children, Irish poet Cecil Frances Alexander wrote poetic verse that made it easier for children to learn the great doctrines of the Bible expressed in the *Book of Common Prayer* and the Apostles' Creed. Her poems, published in 1848 as *Hymns for Little Children*, she sang each week with the children in her Sunday School class.

Did you notice? Mrs. Alexander's much-loved Christmas carol, "Once in royal David's city," is all about children! Jesus as an infant child and "throughout his wondrous childhood," his childhood the pattern and model for all children; Jesus was "little, weak, and helpless," just like your baby brother or sister. He knew firsthand what it meant to be a newborn, a toddler, an eight-year-old, a teenager. And he knows your tears and smiles, your sadness, and what makes you glad. He experienced everything you experience, "yet without sin" (Hebrews 4:15). And through all the stages of childhood, and adulthood, Jesus honored and obeyed his parents. And so must you!

Mrs. Alexander is speaking to children throughout the whole carol! "Christian children all should be/Mild, obedient, good as he." It is because of Jesus' "own redeeming love" that he alone will lead his children to heaven where he rules and reigns at his Father's right hand. She concludes, "When like stars his children crowned," all clothed in white, we will gaze in wonder at King Jesus in all his heavenly splendor—and for all eternity!

Mrs. Alexander's carol has been set to a near-perfect English tune composed by Henry John Gauntlett. Gauntlett got an early start playing and composing music. He became the first organist at St. Peter's and St. Paul's in John Newton's parish church in Olney in England—when he was only nine-years-old! In his adulthood, Gauntlett became such an accomplished organist that composer Felix Mendelssohn chose Gauntlett as the organist to accompany the composer's famous oratorio "Elijah."

I'm told there's a tradition at King's College Cambridge that on Christmas when the boy choristers assemble in the fan-vaulted splendor of the college chapel to sing this carol, none of the boys know who the conductor will select to sing the solo on the opening verse until moments before they sing. Each boy has to be ready.

Imagine if the conductor pointed at you—and you would be the soloist!

### Music of immortal words

A great appreciator of the rural beauty of Ireland, Cecil Frances Alexander also wrote the well-loved hymn "All Things Bright and Beautiful," celebrating God's creation and calling us to praise him for "each little flower that growth," and all things. Later, author James Harriet borrowed the opening phrases of this hymn for the titles of a series of charming books about being a veterinarian in the dales of Yorkshire, England.

Mrs. Alexander wrote some of the tenderest of our hymns, this carol one of her best-loved. Born in Dublin in 1818, she eventually married an Anglican minister who would become the archbishop of the Church of Ireland.

After her death in 1895, her grieving husband said, "The theologian is for the educated few; the preacher is for one generation; the hymn writer speaks an imperishable language." Honoring his beloved wife, he concluded that, "The prophetess, who is also a poet, bequeaths to all the ages the music of immortal words."

The truth of the Bible never changes from age to age, and when biblical truth is adorned by gifted poets in hymns and carols, those who love the truth will always love the hymns in every age.

### Looking more closely

In this carol, Mrs. Alexander helps us get closer to answering the question, what makes a particular kind of hymn a carol? We all know it when we hear it, when we feel it. We hear the opening lines of "Once in royal David's city," and we are transported, gazing awe-struck from the hillsides surrounding that royal city, riveted with wonder at what we are hearing. But what exactly is it we are hearing? Certainly, we are hearing the objective lyrics, the words, the meaning of those words, a place, a royal place, David's city, a faraway and ancient village, a cattle shed, a maiden mother, a little child, a livestock manger for his crib—words of high mystery and with grand historic and redemptive significance.

Wonder of wonders, all this really happened! Jesus Christ was that humble mother's child! Had we been there, we would have seen him, heard him coo and cry—we'd have been beside ourselves with the miracle of it all. But one day, we really will see him, but longer "in this poor lowly stable," we will behold him with new eyes, "Set at God's right hand on high!" For all those Christ came to earth to redeem, on that great day, as the carol has it, "...our eyes at last shall see him"!

**For discussion**

1. Read Micah 5:2-4. What kind of town was David's city Bethlehem. Was it important? Was it big? Why do you think God ordained for his Son Jesus to be born in a town like Bethlehem?
2. Read back through the carol in its poetic lines. What are the character qualities of Jesus that Mrs. Alexender wants children to emulate?
3. The author of this carol tells us that it is through Jesus' "own redeeming love" that we can be like him, and we can at last go to heaven to live with

him forever. Discuss the specific things Jesus accomplished by his redeeming love for his children, things not necessarily included in this carol.

4. How would you feel if you were in the children's choir and, without knowing ahead of time, the conductor pointed at you to sing the solo first stanza of "Once in royal David's city"?
5. Imagine Jesus as an infant, as a toddler, as an adolescent, as a teenager, as an adult. In what ways would you like to be more like Jesus at each of these stages of your life?
6. Now, sing this marvelous carol together as a family!

**Joy to the World**
Isaac Watts (1674-1748)
(December 4)

Joy to the world! The Lord is come:
Let earth receive her King;
Let every heart prepare him room,
And heav'n and nature sing,
And heav'n and nature sing,
And heav'n, and heav'n and nature sing.

Joy to the earth! The Savior reigns:
Let men their songs employ;
While fields and floods, rocks, hills, and plains
Repeat the sounding joy,
Repeat the sounding joy,
Repeat, repeat the sounding joy.

No more let sins and sorrows grow,
Nor thorns infest the ground;

He comes to make his blessings flow
Far as the curse is found,
Far as the curse is found,
Far as, far as the curse is found.[i]

He rules the world with truth and grace,
And makes the nations prove
The glories of his righteousness
And wonders of his love,
And wonders of his love,
And wonders, wonders of his love.

If there is a poetic gene, young Isaac Watts, author of "Joy to the World," had it! Surrounded by the Bible in a godly home, Watts learned poetry from both his sea-captain grandfather and his own gifted father. The boy got an early start with creating poetry on biblical themes; he had been speaking poetry almost as soon as he could talk.

**Childhood rhyming**

His parents were amazed at their boy's oral ability to rhyme spontaneously long before he could write. At first, they encouraged his rhyming—at first. Until young Watts began speaking in rhyme and meter far too often, including replying to his father's questions in their homeschool in poetic couplets. Annoyed by the incessant rhyming, his father had had enough. He may have said something like, "No more rhymes, and I mean it!" Though he really tried, Isaac soon forgot and fell back into rhyming. Taking him over his knee, Watts Sr. prepared to lay into Isaac's backside with the switch. Young Watts cried:

O father, do some mercy take,
And I will no more verses make.

His father did some mercy take that day, and the church can be grateful that Watts, contrary to his childish resolve, continued to make verses of poetry throughout the remainder of his life. The very gift that so annoyed his parents when he was a child would be sanctified and become the means of enriching the worship of thousands of Christians in his lifetime, and millions in the centuries since his death.

**Psalms about Jesus**

In young Watts' day, it was only allowable to sing strict Psalm versifications in church. Doing so began to trouble him. As a poet, many of the English versifications of Psalms sounded lyrically awkward to his sensitive ear. Still more troubling to him, however, was the absence of the name of Jesus in the strict Psalm versifications. Imagine going to church and never singing the name of Jesus! Watts began to ask himself: "Why may we no longer sing of Christ as God? When Christ makes all things new, why must our praises remain in the Old Covenant?"

Encouraged to do something about it by his brother Enoch, Watts began working on a project, *The Psalms of David Imitated in the Language of the New Testament.* Watts wanted the Old Testament to be understood in light of its fulfillment in Christ. "Where the Psalmist . . . talks of sacrificing goats or bullocks, I rather choose to mention the sacrifice of Christ, the Lamb of God." He believed that since all the Scriptures point to Christ, "...going back again to the Jewish forms of worship, and the language of types and figures" in corporate singing was a dishonor to Christ. The best preachers in Watts' day and in ours preach Christ in all the Scriptures, so why shouldn't we *sing* of Christ in the Psalms and all the Scriptures?

**Looking more closely**

When Isaac Watts wrote and published (1719) "Joy to the World," he wasn't intentionally writing a Christmas carol; you might call it an accidental carol! It was intended to be his poetic paraphrase of Psalm 98. But it became a carol, an anthem of rejoicing, a "new song" (98:1) with which to "Make a joyful noise to the Lord" (98:4a). Carols are about joy at the coming of the Son of God in his first Advent (his first coming).

Watts announces in the second phrase, "The Lord is come." He then calls us to make way for the King, "Let every heart prepare him room." Watts' lyric, perhaps by unintended allusion, has prepared us to think of Jesus' humble birth in a cattle stable because there was no room for Mary and Joseph to stay in the inn. No room for Jesus? We must all make room for Jesus!

The rest of the poem is far more about Christ's second Advent, "Let earth receive her King," and "The Savior reigns," and "He rules the world with truth and grace." Of course, Jesus rules and reigns even now, and even in the manger in Bethlehem, but there is a future and final fulfillment of his reign, wherein he will "...make the nations prove/The glories of his righteousness/And wonders of his love." One day the nations' every knee will bow, and every tongue confess (will prove), that Jesus is King of kings, and Lord of lords.

Watts' Psalm 98 is a carol anthem that looks forward to the promised reign of King Jesus over all the earth. Combined with a tune derived from G. F. Handel, "Joy to the World" is one of the best-loved Christmas carols in the English language. Watts invites all people, indeed, all things—"And heaven and nature sing!"—to join him in exuberant wonder at the stupendous salvation God has accomplished for sinners in his Son who has come at last! And Watts' wonder is infectious, as the enduring popularity of this psalm-turned-carol attests.

**For discussion**

1. Read and compare the text of Psalm 98 with the poetry in Watts' carol.
2. Find words and phrases in the psalm and then find how Watts' expresses those ideas in the carol.
3. What are the two most specific Christmas references in Watts' carol? What else might connect this poem to Christmas?
4. "Let every heart prepare him room." Discuss ways that you can prepare room for Jesus in your heart and life this Advent season.
5. The compelling response evoked by Watts' poetry is wonder. What do you think the phrase "exuberant wonder" means? How can you cultivate more wonder at the person and work of Jesus?

**In the Bleak Mid-Winter**

Christina Rossetti (1830-1894)
Gustav Holst (1874-1934)
(December 5)

In the bleak mid-winter
Frosty wind made moan,
Earth stood hard as iron,
Water like a stone;
Snow had fallen, snow on snow,
Snow on snow,
In the bleak mid-winter
Long ago.

Our God, heaven cannot hold him
Nor earth sustain;
Heaven and earth shall flee away
When he comes to reign:
In the bleak mid-winter
A stable-place sufficed

The Lord God Almighty,
Jesus Christ.

Enough for him, whom cherubim
Worship night and day,
A breastful of milk
And a mangerful of hay;
Enough for him, whom angels
Fall down before,
The ox and ass and camel
Which adore.

Angels and archangels
May have gathered there,
Cherubim and seraphim
Thronged the air,
But only his mother
In her maiden bliss,
Worshipped the Beloved
With a kiss.

What can I give him,
Poor as I am?
If I were a shepherd
I would bring a lamb,
If I were a wise man
I would do my part,
Yet what I can I give him,
Give my heart.

**About the poet**

Born December 5 in 1830 (that's today, if you're reading this according to the Advent calendar), Christina Rossetti was the youngest child of an Italian, an exiled poet/scholar living in London. Christina was surrounded by extraordinarily talented parents and siblings.

Her mother, Frances Rossetti, had a significant influence on her children, and on Christina's poetry; she read aloud daily with her children, mostly from the Bible and John Bunyan's *The Pilgrim's Progress*.

Like Isaac Watts before her, Christina began "writing" poetry before she could even write. No doubt daily hearing the Word of God and Bunyan's classic allegory contributed greatly. The first two lines of her first poem give us a peek at a little girl coping with her childhood fears: "Cecilia never went to school/Without her gladiator."

Of the four Rossetti children, Christiana was most like her brother Dante (their father was a scholar of Dante, the author of *Divine Comedy*). She and Dante were dubbed the "two storms" by their father, who correspondingly called her siblings Maria and William the "two calms." Christina was hot-tempered, threw tantrums, and even flew into a rage once and hurt herself with a pair of scissors. But as she matured, she practiced more and more self-control. As an adult, she once counseled her strong-willed niece, "You must not imagine, my dear girl, that your aunt was always the calm and sedate person you now behold. I, too, had a very passionate temper; but I learnt to control it." She continued, describing ways she would "vent my wrath. I have learnt since to control my feelings." She strongly commended doing the same to her niece.

Though she spent most of her life in the bustling city of London, Rossetti loved the countryside. She recollected fondly one of the most important influences on her poetry, "...it was perhaps the delightful idle liberty to prowl all alone about my grandfather's cottage-grounds some thirty miles from London." In this charming setting, Rossetti learned to pay minute attention to the details she found in the natural world, as seen in her carol. She once wrote a tender poem about finding a dead field mouse; she felt it was her duty to give the tiny creature a proper burial.

Encouraged by their mother, the Rossetti children launched a family newspaper, "The Hodge-Podge." During her teen years, Christina and her siblings began playing a poetry game where one of them would propose line endings for a sonnet. Then they would speed write poetry, seeing who could be first to compose the best fourteen lines in the shortest amount of time. Christina dominated this game, sometimes writing an entire sonnet in rhyme and meter in only minutes!

Urged on by her brother Dante, Christina submitted two of her poems to a prestigious literary magazine. To astonished acclaim, both poems were accepted, and she was inaugurated into elite, published-poet status—she was only seventeen!

The most well-known female poet of the era was Elizabeth Barret Browning (much-beloved wife of poet Robert Browning). As Rossetti gained more recognition, comparisons of the two were inevitable. Though

Browning was considered the more academic poet, Rossetti was loved for the things that make poetry—well, poetry! Her brother Dante summed up his sister's skill: "She is the finest woman-poet since Mrs. Browning, by a long way; and in artless art, if not in intellectual impulse, is greatly Mrs. Browning's superior."

Rossetti's skill in "artless art" is on full display in her carol. After the editor of the American literary magazine *Scribner's Monthly* invited readers to send in their best Christmas poems, Rossetti responded and submitted this carol poem. It was published in 1872, though she may have written the carol much earlier.

When it was set to music by composer Gustav Holst in 1906, it went from being a Christmas poem—to being a much-loved Christmas carol, with popular versions recorded by Julie Andrews and James Taylor, and many others.

**Looking more closely**

Rossetti opens her carol with a vivid wintery scene—it even sends chills of snowy cold up the spine. There's not much theological and biblical in the opening stanza, to be honest, though it is evocative poetry, images created with words that awaken our imagination and make us feel what she's writing about—and it may make you shiver with the cold "In the bleak mid-winter"!

Which raises the question of when on the calendar Jesus was actually born. There's vast speculation and theories abound about why we celebrate Jesus' birth in mid-winter, "when the snow lays all about/Deep and crisp and even," at least in some parts of the world.

In the early church, a date emerged for when Jesus was conceived by the Holy Spirit in the womb of the virgin Mary. March 25 became the celebrated date. And if you add nine months, the gestation period for a baby in his mother's womb, you arrive at December 25. The fact is, the Bible doesn't say when on the calendar Jesus was actually born. *That* he was born is without dispute; *when* is far more open to speculation and tradition.

St. Augustine of Canterbury the 6th century missionary to Anglo-Saxon England, established the tradition of celebrating Jesus' birth on December 25. And in the English-speaking world, we've been celebrating Christmas on that date ever since.

Exactly what Rossetti meant by "Heaven cannot hold" Jesus, "Nor earth sustain," is more poetic than clear and denotative. We know from Scripture that Jesus laid aside the glories of heaven to come down to earth to bring about our redemption. We also know that "He sustains all things with the word of his might." In Matthew 24:35, we read that "Heaven and earth will flee away"; Matthew then contrasts this with the eternality of God's Word which abides forever; never passes away; we can count on every word that proceeds from the mouth of God; his Word will never flee away. This is an important truth, one we can count on for all eternity. All the Bible reading that Christina Rossetti's mother did in her childhood paid dividends in her carol.

In the third stanza, Rossetti shifts the lens to the stable scene. It is enough for the Christ child, who was once hailed continually by angel hosts, now to be suckled at his mother's breast, and cradled in "a mangerful of hay." Once angels fell down before him and worshiped continually, but it is enough for him in his incarnation, his coming in the flesh, to be adored by oxen, donkeys, and camels. Rossetti wants us to feel the vast gaping contrast between what Jesus, the Son of God, left behind in celestial glory, for the rustic, earthy stable audience. Angels give way to farm animals! We can almost smell them!

Rossetti is consumed with the mysterious splendor of "Angels and archangels" gathering around to witness the cosmic splendor of the incarnation of the third person of the Triune Godhead, but then, as only a woman could, she wants us to see the scene through the eyes of this teenage virgin mother, bewildered beyond her ability to grasp, but faithful in her calling to be the mother of the Son of God. She is nurturing Jesus with her mother's milk, and united with her infant, he born of her womb, her body giving sustenance to the body of the newborn Son of God, now she does what every mother does over and over again—on her infant son's chubby cheek, she plants a kiss.

In the final stanza, Rossetti muses about gifts. One of the things children love about Christmas is giving and receiving gifts. We wrap them up in shiny paper, festooned with ribbons and bows; we place them under the Christmas tree; sometimes when you think no one is looking, you pick up your gift and shake it, listening, trying to figure out what might be inside.

In her final stanza, Rossetti ponders what kind of gift she, "Poor as I am," can give to Jesus. She's not a shepherd with spare lambs to give him, nor is she a wisemen bringing rich gifts. What can she, what can *you*, give to Jesus this Advent season—and all your life? He came down to earth to do the most difficult task ever given to a son to do—and he did it, perfectly. What can Christina give him? What can you, what can I, give him? "Give my heart." Which is just another way of saying, give Jesus everything I am and have. We owe that. He deserves that.

**For discussion**

1. In the opening stanza of the carol, how many times does Rossetti repeat the word "snow"? Read together Isaiah 1:18 and discuss what snow represents in this Bible verse. Do you think the poet intended to hint at this passage of Scripture?
2. Discuss what you think Christina's brother meant when he referred to her poetry as "artless art." Have you ever seen or heard someone who seemed to be overly full of himself about his artwork?
3. Should Christians ever produce "Art for art's sake"? Or anything else for its own sake—or for the aggrandizement of the one making or doing the thing, whether poetry or music, sermons or septic tanks, collard greens or Christmas carols?
4. Christmas is marked by the giving and receiving of gifts. When you're young, it's easier to prefer the receiving of gifts. What gift does Rossetti want to offer Jesus?
5. The Apostle Paul calls Jesus "the indescribable gift" (II Corinthians 9:15). Why do you think we give gifts at Christmas time? Discuss what it

means to give your heart as a gift back to Jesus for giving himself for you?

**I Heard the Bells on Christmas Day**

Henry Wadsworth Longfellow (1807-1882)

(December 6)

I heard the bells on Christmas Day
Their old, familiar carols play,
   And wild and sweet
   The words repeat
Of peace on earth, good-will to men!

And thought how, as the day had come,
The belfries of all Christendom
   Had rolled along
   The unbroken song
Of peace on earth, good-will to men!

Till ringing, singing on its way,
The world revolved from night to day,
   A voice, a chime,

A chant sublime
Of peace on earth, good-will to men!

And in despair I bowed my head;
"There is no peace on earth," I said;
"For hate is strong,
And mocks the song
Of peace on earth, good-will to men!"

Then pealed the bells more loud and deep:
"God is not dead, nor doth He sleep;
The Wrong shall fail,
The Right prevail,
With peace on earth, good-will to men."

**A famous poet**

Henry Wadsworth Longfellow is arguably the most famous American poet of all time. After reading his much-loved poem written in 1863, "Christmas Bells," do you think it qualifies as a Christmas carol? Most Christians would agree that "Rudolf the red-nosed reindeer," "I'm dreaming of a white Christmas," "Frosty the snowman," don't really qualify as hymns about Jesus' Advent; they're not true Christmas carols. These songs fall more in the genre of seasonal jingles and represent more of the residual fluff that has emerged to pad midwinter with a sort of vague nippy charm, but something is significantly missing for them to rank as true carols.

But how about Longfellow's "Christmas Bells"? Though it is an intriguing poem with a tragic story behind it, is it a true carol?

## The story of "Christmas Bells"

Consider the story behind the poem. While dining in the family home in Cambridge, Massachusetts, December 1, 1863, Longfellow received a telegram. His eldest son had been severely wounded fighting in the Mine Run Campaign of the Civil War. Distraught at the news, Longfellow boarded a train for Virginia. So many men injured in battle, soon after, died in agony from their wounds. He had to be with his son.

This was far from the first woe to descend upon the Longfellow household. Less than two years previous, July 9, 1861, Longfellow had awakened suddenly from a nap. His heart filled with dread. He smelled smoke in the house. Then he heard his wife's voice. Fannie was screaming. He ran into the room; his wife's dress was engulfed in flames.

Frantically, Longfellow tried to smother the fire, finally hurling his own body on his wife. But it was too late. Fannie died the next morning. Longfellow's own burns were so serious he was unable to attend his beloved wife's funeral. For the rest of his life, he wore a beard to conceal the facial scars from his failed attempt to save her life. At times, his grief was so intense, he feared he might need to be confined in an insane asylum.

And now, another blow. Lonely widower with six children, what he feared had come upon him. In the war ripping the country apart, a lead bullet had passed through his eldest son's back and nicked his spine. Would he survive? If he did, would he be paralyzed for life?

**Writing the poem**

Friday, December 25, 1863, anxious for his son, Longfellow listened to the church bells of Cambridge ringing, and the voices of carolers singing "Peace on earth, good-will toward men." The heavy-hearted, fifty-seven-year-old widower, took up his quill and wrote the poem "Christmas Bells." Longfellow penned two other stanzas, not included in hymnals, that are reflective of the poet's misery over the Civil War rending "the hearth-stones of a continent," a war that had nearly taken his son's life only weeks before.

Then from each black, accursed mouth
The cannon thundered in the South,
  And with the sound
  The carols drowned
Of peace on earth, good-will to men!

It was as if an earthquake rent
The hearth-stones of a continent,
  And made forlorn
  The households born
Of peace on earth, good-will to men!

The entire carol invites us to hear, to listen, with Longfellow: to the bells, to the carols, to the cannons thundering. And then to ponder the injustices and griefs of a world very much not at peace, and with little evidence of good will toward other men—much like our world today.

**Is this a real carol?**

In 1872, English organist, John Baptist Calkin, composed the contemplative tune *Waltham* specifically for Longfellow's poem; it's a tune that makes you think deeply as you sing or listen. The best hymnals, however, do not include "Christmas Bells." The reason? There is something, or Someone, conspicuously missing in the lyric. Though the poem alludes to the angels' announcement of the birth of Jesus, the Christ child himself is missing. His absence in Longfellow's poem is problematic. How can it be a Christmas carol when there's nothing about Jesus in the poem?

Does it even qualify as a Christmas carol? There are truths in it: Hate is still tragically strong and does indeed mock the song of peace on earth good-will to men. But is it really a Christmas—a Christ worship—carol? Though the cannons of the Civil War were nearly drowning out the chimes of the Christmas bells in 1863, we can applaud Longfellow for refusing to give in to utter despair. But "hate is strong," and wars abound, persistently so. So, why not despair? Longfellow takes a significant leap between the last two stanzas of his carol, and concludes, as bad as things are, "God is not dead, nor doth He sleep;/The wrong shall fail,/The right prevail."

## The Longfellow gap

But how did he get to that conclusion? I think a genuine Christmas carol, a hymn in praise of Jesus coming into the world as a baby for the sole purpose, "...to save his people from their sins," is the essential truth that is missing, the truth that fills in the gap between Longfellow's deep despair and his final inexplicable confidence that the right will somehow prevail over the wrong expressed in the last stanza, against all evidence.

Is hope merely a delusion? What, or rather, Whom, bridges the gap between the despair and the hope? Maybe we need to look to the rest of the canon of carols to fill that gap. But clearly Longfellow is missing the gospel of grace, that Jesus was born to set his people free, to save us by giving us his life, dying in our place, for our sins. This is a tragic omission.

Without Christ's redeeming work, hope is merely the opiate of the masses, a mind-numbing drug that makes life in a meaningless and miserable world somewhat bearable. But hope isn't a delusion—if our hope is in the Christ of Christmas. With Christ we have every reason for confidence and hope in this life and in the life to come. I wonder if we shouldn't help Longfellow and sing something more like this for the last stanza:

"And then I saw why right prevails!
God's sovereign purpose never fails;
    The Christ child came,
    His sheep to claim,
With peace on earth good-will to men."

**For discussion**

1. Longfellow, as a master poet, awakens our imagination by appealing to our senses, particularly our sense of hearing. Read and discuss the specific things he calls us to hear in this poem. Can you hear them?

2. In literary history, he is known as a Transcendental Optimist, someone who believed that life has meaning, and is worth living, and things will work out in the end. We can't know his heart, but from this poem, do you think Longfellow was a true Christian?
3. Have you had tragedy in your family or in the lives of others you know? Can you identify with Longfellow's sadness expressed in this poem?
4. Read Luke 2:14 and its context. Longfellow was quoting from the King James Bible when he wrote, "peace on earth good-will to men." Compare the English Standard Version of the angels' announcement. "Glory to God in the highest, and on earth peace among those with whom he is pleased." Discuss the difference.

**What Child is This?**

William Chatterton Dix (1837-1865)

(December 7)

What Child is this who, laid to rest,
On Mary's lap is sleeping?
Whom angels greet with anthems sweet,
While shepherds watch are keeping?
This, this is Christ the King,
Whom shepherds guard and angels sing;
Haste, haste to bring him laud,
The Babe, the Son of Mary.

Why lies he in such mean estate,
Where ox and ass are feeding?
Good Christians, fear, for sinners here
The silent Word is pleading.
Nails, spear shall pierce him through,
The cross be borne for me, for you;

Hail, hail the Word made flesh,
The Babe, the Son of Mary.

So bring him incense, gold, and myrrh,
Come peasant, king to own him;
The King of kings salvation brings,
Let loving hearts enthrone him.
Raise, raise a song on high,
The virgin sings her lullaby;
Joy, joy for Christ is born,
The Babe, the Son of Mary.

I love how poet William Chatterton Dix ends each stanza of this carol calling us to worship; "Haste, haste to bring him laud." Laud is an English word transliterated from Latin, and means praise. "Hail, hail the Word made flesh." Hail was a word used to call attention to something, to salute, to greet someone enthusiastically. And then the poet invites us to raise a song and join in singing with Mary's lullaby, "Joy, joy for Christ is born."

**The poet and the music**

Most hymns and carols are written by pastors, men with rich biblical and theological training and understanding. Many are written by the wives of such men, who themselves, in their own right, knew their Bibles and Christian theology. And usually hymns and carols are written by men and women, like Christina Rossetti, who have formal literary training and gifts.

William Chatterton Dix was an exception. He was born in Bristol, England, near the Welsh border, and was the son of a medical doctor. Trained in business, Dix spent much of his life in Glasgow, Scotland working for a maritime insurance company. It is important to remember, however, that educated people in his day had much more training in literature, poetry, music, and theology than in our day.

In 1865, twenty-nine-year-old Dix experienced a severe illness that nearly took his life. His recovery was grindingly slow, and he was plagued with bouts of deep depression. It was in this low condition that the Spirit of God regenerated his sinful heart. He underwent a true gospel awakening that forever changed his life and priorities. He met the "Babe, the son of Mary," "Christ the King." It was in 1865 while recovering that Dix began seriously reading his Bible. Now, saturated in "the Word made flesh," he wrote "What Child is this?"

While living in Scotland, and surrounded by folk music and instruments, he developed a deeper appreciation of music. He was especially taken with the 16th-century melody "Greensleeves." Some musicologists (experts who study music) credit King Henry VIII for composing the much-loved English folk tune. Knowing that in order to be sung, his poetry would need to be in the same meter as its tune, Dix wrote his carol to fit the existing meter of "Greensleeves."

Dix wrote other carols and hymns, considered to be imaginative, reverent, and simple. "What Child is this?" was first published in 1871 in a celebrated collection entitled, "*Christmas Carols, Old and New.*" It has become a favorite carol in +++the English-speaking (and singing) world.

## Looking more closely

Dix begins the carol with a question in the opening line. We might be tempted to scoff at the question. What Child is this? This is Christmas. Doesn't everybody know who the Child is? Poet's sometimes use rhetorical questions, ones many of us know or think we know the full answer to already. Isaac Watts does the same in one of his great hymns, "Why was I made to hear his voice/And enter while there's room?" The only answer is because of the inexplicable free grace and mercy of our sovereign God. Why me? The only fitting response is gratitude, love, and praise, a lifetime of awe-struck doxology.

Here, Dix employs the rhetorical question to create a similar sense of wonder, of awe at the uniqueness of this Child. What Child is this? Children were born all the time in the ancient near-eastern world. What's so special about this one? "This, this is Christ the King," the Son of God, the only Savior of sinners, the long-promised Messiah, here at last! The Christ child is so much more than simply another baby born in the city of David. Because of that, the poet invites us to hail him, to make haste to bring him laud and honor, the only fitting response to such a Child as this.

Notice how the poet creates a contrast between the splendor of the angelic hosts—a phalanx of celestial warriors—by conveying their heavenly message to insignificant shepherds, the lowest occupation of the day. This Child is hailed by angels singing "anthems sweet," but in stark contrast, guarded and watched over by shepherds; lowly illiterate peasants of no account, the riff-raff of society, yet Jesus will call himself the Good Shepherd who had come to lay down his life for the sheep.

Our poet then asks another question in stanza two. Why is such a heavenly Child, born of a poor virgin mother, placed in the feeding trough of oxen, sheep, and donkeys? Why not have him born in the pomp and grandeur of a palace, surrounded by the wealthy, the influential, senators and statesman, the important people of society? But here he is, cradled alongside common farm animals in his birth? Imagine the smells. I've raised cattle on our family farm. There are lots of sounds and smells. "Why lies he in such mean estate?" Why such a lowly and smelly entrance into the world?

Because of what he had come to do. What Child is this? To answer the question further, Dix wants us to project forward into the deeper reasons for the incarnation of the second person of the Trinity. It was coming. Jesus came to undergo the ignominy of the cross, the nails driven into his feet and hands; the spear thrust into his side. Far from this being a distraction from the pastoral scene unfolding before our eyes, the newborn baby cooing in his mother's embrace. No, the poet wants us to see the larger meaning behind it all—as he had come to know the gospel himself.

This Child's "mean estate" is a foreshadowing of his coming suffering, being stricken, smitten, and afflicted—the Lamb to be slaughtered for the sins of his people. Dix doesn't want a merely sentimental image in our minds' eyes. He wants us to contemplate deeply what Child is this? Who he is and the awful task he has come to accomplish, "The cross be borne for me, for you."

With such a mission and purpose lying ahead for this Child, the poet compels us to worship, "Hail, hail, the Word made flesh."

Next, the poet conflates the wisemen into this scene (who will come as much as two years later), the three kings from the east, who came to worship the Child, to shower him with rich gifts, fitting for "The King of kings" who is bringing salvation. Loving hearts will enthrone such a Child as this; they will "Raise, raise a song on high."

Along with Mary's lullaby to her newborn son, all loving hearts will want to sing with "Joy, joy for Christ is born"! You can be among those loving hearts this day, throughout this Advent season—and forevermore!

**For discussion**

1. Read John 1:1-14 and discuss what it means that Jesus was the Word made flesh.
2. In order for Mr. Dix to craft such a beautiful carol, what were some things he needed to learn, and what changes needed to happen in his heart and life before he was able to write this fine carol?
3. Can you think of others who God brought through great illness and depression to a living faith in Christ?
4. Discuss together what the phrase "Let loving hearts enthrone him" means. What kind of people sit on thrones? Jesus is the King of kings

already seated at his Father's right hand, seated on his throne. If he's already sitting on his throne in heaven, in what sense are we invited to "enthrone" him?

5. Now, as a family, join your voices with Mr. Dix's and "Raise, raise a song on high."

**Let All Mortal Flesh Keep Silence**

Gerard Moultrie (1829-1885)

Liturgy of St. James (AD 275)

(December 8)

Let all mortal flesh keep silence,
And with fear and trembling stand;
Ponder nothing earthly-minded,
For with blessing in his hand,
Christ our God to earth descendeth,
Our full homage to demand.

King of kings, yet born of Mary,
As of old on earth he stood,
Lord of lords, in human vesture,
In the body and the blood;
He will give to all the faithful
His own self for heav'nly food.

Rank on rank the host of heaven
Spreads its vanguard on the way,

As the Light of light descendeth
From the realms of endless day,
That the pow'rs of hell may vanish
As the darkness clears away.

At his feet the six-winged seraph,
Cherubim with sleepless eye,
Veil their faces to the presence,
As with ceaseless voice they cry:
"Alleluia, Alleluia
Alleluia, Lord Most High!"

**The oldest carol**

"Let all mortal flesh keep silence" is likely the very oldest of our Christmas carols—except Mary's inspired Magnificat, Zechariah's song, Simeon's song, and what the angels actually said in song to the shepherds at Jesus birth! This carol was originally composed in Greek, the language the New Testament was written in, to be sung in the Liturgy of St. James, but some hymnologist (experts who study hymns) believe it predates that liturgy and was first written and sung as early as 275 AD. Imagine yourself joining your voice and singing with Christians who lived more than 1,800 years ago! That's way older than your mom and dad, or even your grandparents!

One of the things I particularly appreciate about the origins of this carol/hymn is that in a church tradition where eventually experts did almost all of the singing and the congregation just passively observed, and listened in on the beautiful singing, this carol was intended for the whole congregation to sing—children included! It was called a Cherubic Hymn, that is a hymn for cherubs, or angels, to sing. This carol was symbolically an invitation for the ordinary worshiper, like you and me, to join the choir of angels singing around God's throne in heaven. Isn't that wonderful?

Early church father John Chrysostom (b. 347 AD) put it this way in a short sermon, "On high, the armies of angels give glory; below, men, standing in church forming a choir, emulate the same doxologies. Above, the Seraphim declaim the thrice-holy hymn; below, the multitude of men sends up the same. A common festival of the heavenly and the earthly is celebrated together; one [thanksgiving], one exultation, one joyful choir."

You and your family get to join in singing with this heavenly choir in your family worship this evening! Can you sing like an angel? If you fix your eyes and heart on Jesus, seated on his throne, at his Father's right hand, you will sing with a heart bursting with love and adoration to the great Savior who came to save his people—moms and dads, and brothers and sisters—from their sins. One day we really will sing around that throne with the angelic hosts. Let's practice tonight and give him glory!

**A word about the music**

The English composer and musical enthusiast Ralph Vaughan Williams is credited with discovering the tune and arranging it in 1906 to be sung with this ancient carol. Williams discovered the folk tune in a region in France just north of Paris; people had been singing the tune at the baker's oven or the blacksmith's anvil for centuries, but it had never been written down before Williams heard the tune, set it to musical notation, and named it *Picardy*.

Picardy was the region where Williams first heard peasants singing the tune, and where John Calvin was born in 1509 in a cathedral village called Noyon-le-saint, just Noyon today. Calvin would be used of God as the most careful theologian of the Protestant Reformation. *Picardy* is a marvelous melody, well suited to accompany this angelic carol for everyone to sing in the worship of Jesus.

*Picardy* is composed in a minor key, so it sounds sober, breathless, and hushed—as if the angels in heaven were singing with awe and wonder the profound and beautiful words set to this music.

**Looking more closely**

Once again, this poem was translated from Greek into English by a very able scholar and poet, Gerard Moultrie. He studied at Exeter College, Oxford in the 1850s, the same college where young J. R. R. Tolkien would later be a student. As with any poetry translated and versified, that is, put into rhyme and meter in English, we owe Mr. Moultrie a great debt for his skillful poetic work.

The opening stanza of this carol is ironic, that is it seems to be telling us to be silent, but we're also supposed to be singing. That's an example of something that is ironic. The opening line comes straight from the pages of the Bible in Habakkuk 2:20, where the prophet wrote, "Let all the earth keep silence before [God]." Also, the prophet Zechariah

(2:13) wrote, "Be silent, all flesh, before the Lord, for he has roused himself from his holy dwelling." Moultrie the poet might also have been thinking of Isaiah 6 when the prophet saw the Lord, and in terror, with "fear and trembling," fell on his face before God.

Why the silence? Why the fear and trembling? Why the poetry and music that seems too wonderful to take on our lips? In the presence of Jesus, we would be hushed with awe and reverence, don't you think?

We're also urged to "ponder nothing early minded," that is, if we were in the presence of God himself, do you think you would be caring about whether your mom will make mac-n-cheese or peanut-butter-and-jelly sandwiches for lunch, or who will win the baseball game on Friday? There's nothing wrong with lunch and baseball, but if Jesus descended to earth to meet with you personally, to bless you with his love and salvation, you would want to bring your "full homage," that is, your full worship and adoration of him; by comparison, nothing else on earth would have any importance; nothing else on this earth could keep you from joining the angels in falling at the feet of Jesus and calling him "Lord Most High!" And here's another wonderful thing, when worshiping Jesus matters more to you than any earthly thing, *every* earthly thing suddenly takes on the most stupendous importance!

In the second stanza, another irony is introduced, two things that just seem not to go together. Jesus was "King of kings, yet born of Mary"! How could this be? God born to a poor teenage virgin from a backwater, no-account town? He was "Lord of lords," but was now a flesh-and-blood baby, wearing a human form, and he had come to give his body and blood, for our salvation. How could this be?

When your pastor and elders serve the Lord's Supper at your church, you are reminded of Jesus' flesh and blood sacrificed for your sins. He gave himself and nourishes us with himself as if he were heavenly food! What do we do when something is amazing beyond words? Well, we "let all mortal flesh keep silence!"

But then, enter the angels! Don't think of angels as fleshy effeminate cartoon characters. Think celestial Navy Seals. In the third stanza we meet "Rank on rank the host of heaven." These are angelic warriors, a host, a vast army spreading their wings, falling in reverence before the "Light of light," Jesus himself come to clear away the darkness, to vanquish, to conquer, "the powers of hell." He does it with his warrior messengers, not chubby cherubs with little wings!

And still more angels! In the fourth stanza we meet angels that are so busy worshiping King Jesus that they never sleep! But Jesus' light is so stupendously wonderful, it's like trying to look at the sun (don't try this), so bright is his light that they veil their faces with their wings. And then they break into unending singing, "with ceaseless voice they cry: 'Alleluia,'" three times over, for Father, Son, and Holy Spirit, "'Lord Most High!'"

Don't you want to join in, sing with these warrior angels? Sing with almost 2,000 years of other boys and girls, and whole families singing? I certainly do!

**For discussion**

1. Look up in your Bible and read together Habakkuk 2:20 and Zechariah 2:13. You might want to read the context of each passage, and then discuss similarities with this carol.
2. What are other things that are ironic? We sometimes call ironic things, counter-intuitive things, things that at first don't seem to go together. What are other things in the Bible and in the gospel, the Good News of Jesus Christ, that are ironic? Talk about this.
3. Do you think it's important to join your voice with Christian boys and girls and whole families down through the millennia, and with angels, singing carols to King Jesus? Why is that important for the church to do today?
4. Contrast this high-register carol with "Rudolph, the red-nosed reindeer." Discuss the differences as a family. What kind of music do you think the angels are singing ceaselessly to the Triune God in heaven right now?
5. What do you feel going on inside of you when you sing, "Let all mortal flesh keep silence," to the French folk melody, *Picardy*? Can you express it in words?

**O Come, O Come, Emmanuel**

Latin Antiphons, 12th century
Translated and versified by
John Mason Neale (1818-1866)
(December 9)

O come, O come, Emmanuel,
And ransom captive Israel;
That mourns in lonely exile here,
Until the Son of God appear.
Rejoice! Rejoice! Emmanuel
Shall come to thee, O Israel.

O come, O come, thou Lord of Might
Who to thy tribes, on Sinai's height,
In ancient times didst give the law,
In cloud, and majesty, and awe.
Rejoice! Rejoice! Emmanuel
Shall come to thee, O Israel.

O come, thou Rod of Jesse, free
Thine own from Satan's tyranny;
From depths of hell thy people save,
And give them victory o'er the grave.
Rejoice! Rejoice! Emmanuel
Shall come to thee, O Israel.

O come, thou Day-Spring from on high,
And cheer us by thy drawing nigh;
Disperse the gloomy clouds of night,
And death's dark shadows put to flight.
Rejoice! Rejoice! Emmanuel
Shall come to thee, O Israel.

O come, thou Key of David, come
And open wide our heavenly home;
Make safe the way that leads on high,
And close the path to misery.
Rejoice! Rejoice! Emmanuel
Shall come to thee, O Israel.

**The music**

The Medieval plainsong melody *Veni Emmanuel* is a tune long shrouded in mystery. We know it means "Come, Emmanuel" in English. But who wrote it, and when? British musicologist Mary Berry, solved the mystery. While doing research at the National Library of France in 1966, she discovered a 15th-century manuscript of the tune. Berry dug further; she came to believe that the tune was likely much older. Either way, the sober grandeur of the melody, concluding with a flourish of joy in the refrain, is a fitting accompaniment to John Mason Neale's English versification of the original Latin poetry.

**About the poet**

The biblical ideas explored in the carol came from an ancient Latin antiphon; an antiphon is liturgical poetry (poetry to sing in church) intended to be sung alternately by two different groups of singers, as if responding back and forth to one another in a conversational song. Some hymnologists believe the original Latin poetry was written over 1,000 years ago. But our English version came into being in 1851 from the pen of John Mason Neale, an Anglican minister, Cambridge scholar, and poet.

Neale was part of the Oxford Movement, an influential group who wanted to revert back to Roman Catholic beliefs and rituals and bring these into the Protestant Church. Neale joined many in the movement who wanted to abolish the Anglican Church altogether. Tempers flared during the controversy, even with threats of beating and burning houses down.

Neale did better when he was writing poetry, including "Good King Wenceslaus," a carol celebrating the Bohemian king in Prague, observing a poor man gathering winter fuel in the snow; it's a story carol full of warm midwinter images and emotions, but much less about the meaning of the birth of Christ.

Neale also translated and versified the early church carol by Prudentius, "Of the Father's Love Begotten," with a contemplative Medieval plainsong tune. Prudentius lived at the same time as Augustine of Hippo, the most important and widely read church father by the Reformers of the 16th-century, helping them to rediscover the free grace of the gospel. Neale wrote about Mary's important role in giving birth to Jesus, "the world's Redeemer." But because of the error of his Roman Catholic leanings, he placed unbiblical emphasis on Jesus' mother, quoting a line in the carol from prayers Catholics actually pray to "the virgin full of grace."

**Looking more closely**

In "O come, O come, Emmanuel," however, I can't see anything true believers will disagree with. This carol is a richly biblical prayer, not to Mary, but to Emmanuel, to Jesus, so we can sing these grand lines from our hearts.

Read back over each stanza of this wonderful carol, and let's look more closely at what is going on. Clearly this is carol all about coming, about the Advent of Jesus. Ancient prophets had long foretold the coming of Emmanuel, and the angel had announced to Joseph that he didn't need to figure out a name for his son; Mary's baby boy already had a name! Each stanza of this carol comes white-hot out of many specific texts of God's Word.

In the opening stanza we hear echoes of Isaiah 35:10: "...the ransomed of the Lord will return and come with joyful shouting to Zion, with everlasting joy upon their heads. They will find gladness and joy, and sorrow and sighing will flee away." The promised Son of God has appeared, and he's done so to ransom, to buy, to purchase, God's people Israel from their captivity. All enslaved mourners, those who sigh with sadness, Emmanuel is coming to free you! Rejoice!

In Exodus 19:18, we're told that when Moses went up Mount Sinai, and the "Lord of Might" met him there to reveal his law to the tribes of Israel, the mountain was engulfed "In cloud, and majesty, and awe." There was fire. There was an earthquake. There was smoke—you and I would have fallen on our faces in fright. But, terrible as God's presence seemed, he had actually come "in ancient times [to] give the law"; revealing his will was an important part of God's redemptive plan. But, while the law exposes and restrains our sin, it has no power to deliver us from sin. Only Jesus can do that! Rejoice! Jesus has come! And now, motivated not by the letter of the law, but by our love and gratitude, we walk, we serve, we worship, we live out our lives to the glory of God, by the grace of God alone. Rejoice! Jesus has come to fulfill the law and to lead us into all righteousness.

A host of biblical places had foretold that the Messiah Jesus would be born into the same family line that King David was born into; "Thou Rod of Jesse," Jesse being David's father. And Jesus was coming on a rescue mission, to "free/Thine own from Satan's tyranny," to save his people from "depths of hell," and to give us "victory over the grave," and life eternal. Of course, we must rejoice! Rejoice because Jesus, God with us, has come!

Do you notice the different biblical names for Jesus in these stanzas? In stanza four the poet uses the name "Day-Spring" as if that were an actual name for Jesus; it's the name used in the King James Version of Luke 1:78; it's an old way of saying "sunrise" or "dawn," the morning of redemption has sprung! Here the poet is using the literary devise called personification, referring to the sunrise of redemption as a name "Day-Spring from on high," a name for Jesus. And what does the sunrise do when it cheers us and comes nigh, or near us, when it springs up in the morning? It disperses "the gloomy clouds of night," and puts to flight "death's dark shadows." The morning light drives out the darkness. Rejoice! The Day-Spring is here! Emmanuel has come!

At last, in the final stanza is another name referring to Jesus, who holds the "Key of David." Neale, in collaboration with the unknown Medieval poet, has taken this name right out of Revelation 3:7, where Jesus holds the only key that opens and shuts his dominions and the doors of heaven. With this key, Jesus "open[s] wide our heavenly home," and makes the way safe, "And close[s] the path to misery." Aren't you glad that Jesus holds this key? Again, the poet invites us, twice over, to "Rejoice! Rejoice! Emmanuel" at last has come with his key in hand to unlock the gates of heaven and let us in!

**For discussion**

1. Read together Isaiah 59:10 and discuss similarities with the opening lines of this carol.
2. Read and compare the prophecy in Isaiah 7:4 with what the angel told Joseph in Matthew 1:23. What does Emmanuel mean?
3. The best hymns and carols are full of the Bible, as this carol is. Discuss the different names the

poet uses for Jesus. Can you find any other biblical references or allusions?

4. As you sing this together as a family, can you sense how well the poetry and music go together? It seems like no other music would work!
5. God made us for singing, and for rejoicing! How many Bible references can you think of that tell us to rejoice always?

**God Rest You, Merry Gentlemen**

English Carol, anonymous 17th-century

(December 10)

God rest you, merry gentlemen,
Let nothing you dismay,
Remember Christ our Savior
Was born on Christmas-day
To save poor souls from Satan's power,
When we were gone astray;
O tidings of comfort and joy.

From God our heavenly Father
A blessed angel came,
And unto certain shepherds
Brought tidings of the same,
How that in Bethlehem was born
The Son of God by name:
O tidings of comfort and joy.

“Fear not,” then said the angel,
“Let nothing you affright,
This day is born a Savior
Of virtue, power and might;
To free all those who trust in him
From Satan’s power and might.
O tidings of comfort and joy.”

The shepherds at those tidings
Rejoiced much in mind,
And left their flocks a-feeding
In tempest, storm and wind,
And went to Bethlehem straightway,
This blessed Babe to find:
O tidings of comfort and joy.

### The Gentlemen-nothing song

“Daddy, can we sing the Gentlemen-nothing song?” I was puzzled. In our family worship, I’ve often let my six children pick the hymn we sing together on their night of the week. When young Cedric, with his characteristic full-bodied grin, first made this request, I had no idea what he wanted to sing (he’s now a husband and father with a houseful of young sons himself). “You know the one, Daddy…” and then he began singing, “God rest you merry, gentlemen/Let nothing…” I had to laugh. My son had blended the word “gentlemen” and the word “nothing” into his own boyish title for the carol. I still call this carol the “Gentlemen-nothing song.”

In some people’s minds, this is the quintessential English-feeling carol, and it has appeared as such in various places. Charles Dickens in his 1843 novella *A Christmas Carol*, makes mention of it alongside the miser Ebeneezer Scrooge, and the creators of the perennial favorite *Muppet Christmas Carol* movie include street scenes where carolers are singing the "Gentlemen-nothing song." George Elliot in her 1861 classic *Silas Marner* makes mention of the carol. Not every mention of this carol, however, is complimentary. In the March, 1824 issue of *The Gentleman's Magazine*, a journalist bemoans that no real carols are heard in the streets of London, "excepting some croaking ballad-singer bawling out 'God rest you, merry gentlemen,' or a like doggerel." Not very flattering, as a doggerel is a crude, ill-formed, trite jingle.

What are we to make of "The Gentlemen-nothing song"? Alongside some of the greatest carols included in this volume, it seems to lack some of the depth, the gravitas (the weight), and the majesty. Nevertheless, it has managed to find a place among the much-loved Christmas carols—at least with my son Cedric!

**A word about the music**

The very-English-sounding melody for this carol appeared about the same time as the lyrics, but is also anonymous. The melody for "God rest you, merry gentlemen" was arranged by Samuel Wesley (1766-1837), son of Charles and nephew of John Wesley, both evangelists and prolificate hymn writers. By the time he was eight-years-old, Samuel was well on the way to mastery of the violin and other instruments. He was so gifted, that the musical establishment in London dubbed him a child prodigy on a par with his contemporary

Mozart. His father Charles Wesley wrote of his son, "He was full eight-years-old when Dr. Boyce came to see us and accosted me with, 'Sir, I hear you have an English Mozart in your house.' I called Sam to answer for himself. He had by this time scrawled down his Oratorio of *Ruth*. The Doctor looked it over very carefully and seemed highly pleased with the performance. Some of his words were, 'These airs are some of the prettiest I have seen. This boy writes by nature as true a bass as I can do by rule and study.'"

Not only was Samuel Wesley called the "English Mozart," he also came to be known as the best improvisor on the organ in England, that meant he could take a simple tune and, without looking at the music, play on and on adding and developing his own musical ideas as he played. Though he didn't compose the original tune, he arranged the music to fit with the carol poetry so we can sing it.

**Looking more closely**

We all love a good story. When a story is told in song, we sometimes call it a ballad. This is a ballad carol, each stanza adding new information to the story. The repeated refrain, "O tidings of comfort and joy," reminds us of Luke 2:10 when the angel appeared in the sky to the shepherds, assuring them, telling them to rest easy; there was nothing to dismay them in these tidings. Far from it! The angel had come to announce the birth of "Christ our Savior," who came "To save poor souls from Satan's power."

But what about the "merry gentlemen" phrase? Have you wondered what we mean when we greet others during Advent with "Merry Christmas"? We don't ordinarily use the word "merry" in today's spoken English; it's an archaic word from the past, so we need to define our terms.

"Merry" means delightful, pleasing, cheerful, joyful. It seems to be stronger than the word happy—maybe even closer to blessed. So, the carol opens addressing "merry gentlemen," the shepherds are included, to be sure, but all people, in whatever dismay they find themselves, even the prodigal sons or daughters who've gone astray, who've wandered into the far country. This is a merry message—all who hear are welcomed by the blessed tidings of Christmas and Jesus' birth.

The second stanza further develops the visitation of the blessed angels to the shepherds, sent "from God our heavenly Father," to announce that "in Bethlehem was born/The Son of God by name," tidings of Good News indeed!

I am certain that had you and I been there, we too would have been "affrighted," scared spitless, in fact! So, the angel reassures the frightened shepherds: the Savior had come to use his "power and might/To free all those who trust in him." These were comforting and joyful tidings because Jesus was born to set his people free "From Satan's power and might."

In the final stanza, the shepherds set aside their fear and "Rejoiced much in mind." They left everything to follow Jesus, as we are called to do. Careless of their sheep, left alone feeding out on the hillside, "In tempest, storm, and wind," the shepherds dropped everything to go straightway to Bethlehem to find "The blessed Babe."

These were indeed “tidings of comfort and joy,” tidings worth singing about!

**For discussion**

1. Read back through the carol and summarize the episodes of the ballad, the story being told in the song.
2. You might want to reread the account in Luke 2:8-21 and compare the biblical account with the story being told in this carol.
3. You’ve been learning about and singing other carols with your family during this Advent season. How would you compare this carol with some of the others? Is it a doggerel (look up the word in the dictionary)? Can you give specific reasons for your comparisons?
4. The shepherds left their sheep defenseless out on the hillside. David as a shepherd boy had to fight off a bear and lion to keep them from devouring his sheep. Was it a good idea for the shepherds to leave their sheep?
5. Read together Luke 5:28 and compare with Matthew 4:22 and Luke 9:61. What do these followers of Jesus leave behind? What do you think Jesus wants you to leave behind as you become a follower of him?

**Hark! the Herald Angels Sing**

Charles Wesley (1707-1742)

(December 11)

Hark! The herald angels sing,
"Glory to the newborn King;
Peace on earth, and mercy mild,
God and sinners reconciled!"
Joyful, all ye nations rise,
Join the triumph of the skies;
With th'angelic host proclaim,
"Christ is born in Bethlehem!"

Hark! the herald angels sing,
"Glory to the newborn King!"

Christ, by highest heav'n adored;
Christ the everlasting Lord;
Late in time, behold him come,
Offspring of a virgin's womb.
Veiled in flesh the Godhead see;
Hail th'incarnate Deity,

Pleased with us in flesh to dwell,
Jesus our Emmanuel.

Hark! the herald angels sing,
"Glory to the newborn King!"

Hail the heav'n-born Prince of Peace!
Hail the Sun of Righteousness!
Light and life to all he brings,
Ris'n with healing in his wings.
Mild he lays his glory by,
Born that man no more may die;
Born to raise the sons of earth,
Born to give them second birth.

Hark! the herald angels sing,
"Glory to the newborn King!"

**About the music and composer**

One of the greatest composers of the 1800s, Felix Mendelssohn-Bartholdy (1809-1847), composed the tune for Charles Wesley's fine carol. Born into a Jewish family in Germany, Mendelssohn grew up surrounded by anti-Semitism; hating Jews began long before Adolph Hitler and their extermination by the Nazis. His parents converted to the Reformed faith when he was seven years old, and he was raised in a committed Christian family. He was a musical genius and wrote many fine symphonies and oratorios, *Elijah* being one of his finest.

We also owe Mendelsohn for the rediscovery of another German composer that had almost entirely been forgotten, Johann Sebastian Bach—another committed Christian and my favorite composer of all time. Bach ended all of his composition with the initials SDG, *soli*

*Deo gloria*, to God alone the glory. Bach and Mendelssohn wanted their music—and everything else they accomplished—to give glory to God.

**About the poet**

I'm pretty certain that Charles Wesley also wanted to bring glory to God with his life. Born in 1707, his godly mother Susanna Wesley, gave birth to eighteen other children! "Hark! the Herald Angels Sing," one of the best-loved hymns of all time, was only one of 6,500 hymns Wesley wrote. As an evangelist, he was also passionate for the souls of unbelievers who needed to hear the gospel of Jesus Christ. He traveled many thousands of miles on horseback preaching to the poor and needy around England, Wales, and Ireland, sometimes writing his hymns and carols while jostling along on his horse's back.

Another way Wesley expressed an unusual concern for the downtrodden, was his ministry to condemned prisoners on death row in Bristol and in London. These were men, women, and children condemned to the gallows for even petty crimes. Wesley wanted them to repent of their sins and know the saving grace of Christ—before the noose was tightened around their necks and they were hanged.

After hearing Moravian Christians singing hymns on board ship during a violent storm, Wesley found his own calling as a hymn writer in Psalm 40, "He hath put a new song in my mouth, even praise unto our God: many shall see it, and fear, and shall trust in the Lord."

In one of his finest hymns, Wesley employed a metaphor drawn from his own spiritual bondage and from his time with prisoners chained in dungeons, awaiting their execution:

Long my imprisoned spirit lay
Fast bound in sin and nature's night;
Thine eye diffused a quickening ray,
I woke, the dungeon flamed with light;
My chains fell off, my heart was free;
I rose, went forth, and followed thee.

Here is perhaps the finest poetic summary of the supernatural work of the Spirit of God when he diffuses "a quickening ray" into the heart of an imprisoned sinner. The rescue of one enchained sinner is great cause for rejoicing and for singing, "Glory to the newborn King!"

**Looking more closely**

In the opening lines of Wesley's carol, the poet calls us to attention. He's in earnest and wants us to hear "The herald angels sing." Wesley knew his Bible inside and out; almost every phrase, every line, of this carol comes from the words of Scripture. "The newborn King," was here! He'd come to bring peace and mercy, to make "God and sinners reconciled," no longer enemies but friends. Here is a joyous message for all the nations to rise and sing, and "With the angelic host proclaim/'Christ is born in Bethlehem!'"

In the second stanza, Wesley wants us to feel the slack-jaw wonder of Jesus' preexistence in heaven, adored as God himself from all eternity, without beginning or end; he was "Christ the everlasting Lord." Marvelous things are afoot! In Matthew 1:23, the apostle records from the prophets that "the virgin will conceive and bear a son." An unmarried woman, a true virgin, cannot have a child. Your mother needed to marry your father in order for you to be conceived and then be born as a baby boy or girl. It's wonderful stuff, and someday, you'll understand much more about it.

But Jesus' birth would be like no other. Jesus had no earthly father involved in his conception in Mary's womb. He was conceived by the Holy Spirit, the "Offspring of a virgin's womb." Natural birth is amazing. But Jesus is the second person of the Godhead, now "veiled in flesh," "the incarnate deity." This was stupendously wonderful! Jesus, who was fully deity, that is God, was now incarnate, come in the flesh. His birth was a supernatural miracle, the greatest event in human history!

Wesley continues, making allusions to still more Scripture passages. The last stanza opens, calling us to give honor to "the heaven-born Prince of Peace!" We know the angel announced peace on earth to the shepherds, but in Isaiah 9:6 the prophet foretells that Jesus would be the Prince of Peace. In Malachi 4:2, we read about the Sun of Righteousness rising with healing in his wings. In Philippians, we read about Christ laying aside his glory, and he does so without complaint or chafing, "Mild he lays his glory by." Wesley then concludes with a flurry of three lines explaining why Jesus was born: to conquer death for his people, "to raise the sons of earth" from the corruption and curse of their sin, and "Born to give them second birth." Do you remember what Jesus told Nicodemus when he came to him by night?

**For discussion**

1. The musical composer Mendelsohn and J. S. Bach wanted everything they accomplished to bring glory to God. What are ways you can bring glory to God in your life today?
2. Read John 8:12 where Jesus is talking about who he is and what he had come to bring. Can you find a phrase in the carol that came from this verse of Scripture?
3. There are words in this carol that we don't use in our ordinary daily speech. What does "hark" mean? What does "hail" mean in this context? What do you think "mild" means, used twice in this carol?
4. Read together Isaiah 9:6. What other names does the prophet use for the coming Son of God? Discuss what those names mean.
5. Christmas is all about birth, the birth of Jesus. But Wesley concludes with a reference to another birth. Read John 3:1-7 and discuss the meaning of the final line of the last stanza of Wesley's carol.

**What Wonder Filled the Starry Night**

Douglas Bond (1958-)

(December 12)

What wonder filled the starry night
        When Jesus came with heralds bright!
I marvel at his lowly birth,
        That God for sinners stooped to earth.

His splendor laid aside for me,
        While angels hailed his Deity,
The shepherds on their knees in fright
        Fell down in wonder at the sight.

The child who is the Way, the Truth,
        Who pleased his Father in his youth,
Through all his days the Law obeyed,
        Yet for its curse his life he paid.

What drops of grief fell on the site
        Where Jesus wrestled through the night,
Then for transgressions not his own,
        He bore my cross and guilt alone.

What glorious Life arose that day
        When Jesus took death's sting away!
His children raised to life and light,
        To serve him by his grace and might.

One day the angel hosts will sing,
        "Triumphant Jesus, King of kings!"
Eternal praise we'll shout to him
        When Christ in splendor comes again!

We have been exploring how wonderful Christmas carols are to us, how unique, how the best carols have a particular high-register and endearing quality about them. Have you noticed that the authors of all the carols in this Advent family devotional—are dead? Some of these carols have been around since before the Middle Ages; God's people have been singing these lyrics for centuries, and many of their poets have been dead for a very long time.

**Writing a Christmas carol**

Maybe you've noticed already. There's something unique about this carol. Many of you have never heard of it! Families who have are only from this generation. Nobody sang this carol in the Middle

Ages! Its poet is getting older, but he's not dead—yet. You've figured it out! I began writing it in 2010, not very long ago compared to the rest of these carols. Why on earth would I try to write a Christmas carol?

I was asking myself that very question when the idea first began forming. I wanted a carol that encompassed the grand sweep of redemptive history, from Jesus' first coming in the manger, to the triumphal Second Coming of King Jesus, and all that he accomplished in between. But there's so many wonderful Christmas carols, anyone attempting to write a new one is doomed to failure; the bar is simply too high. But here it is. Do my meagre literary efforts have any hope of measuring up to other carols, the ones that move our hearts, that we love to sing? Only time will tell.

In part because of such fears, early scribblings for this carol sat dormant for several years; hymn writing can sometimes be like that for me, an initial burst of creative ideas, then nothing, just an imaginative black hole. As Christmas approached in 2010, however, something changed. Sitting in front of the fire in our living room one crisp winter evening, after my "children were nestled all snug in their beds," I pulled out the initial notes again. Before my bedtime, I managed to sift through all the scribbles, idea banks and word banks, and, with some trepidation, set down the lines pretty much as you see them here.

Carols are replete with emotive atmosphere, sacred charm, celebratory associations, roasting chestnuts, crackling fires, Christmas stockings hung on the mantle, Jack Frost nipping at our noses, "Good King Wenceslas [going] out/When the snow lay all about," and every cozy winter connotation imaginable (and some unimaginable). So endearing are carols to the full canon of what Christians sing, hymnologists tell us the best-loved hymn of all time is actually a carol, Wesley's "Hark, the Herald Angels Sing."

With the same fear and trembling I had when I originally set my imagination to work on this carol, I offer it to your family, with hopes that it may contribute to a meaningful and Merry Christmas.

**Looking more closely**

In the opening stanza, I wanted to place myself, and any who sing along with me, there in Bethlehem; the "starry night," alluding to the star that would appear later and guide the wisemen to Jesus, the "heralds bright" announcing their angelic song, the marvel of Jesus' "lowly birth," his stooping to earth to rescue sinners.

Think with me at what Jesus laid aside, what splendor in heaven he left behind when he "stooped to earth." The angels knew that splendor, what it cost him; little wonder they "hailed his Deity." Imagine if you were a shepherd watching over your flocks on a quiet Judean hillside that night—and suddenly angel hosts burst resplendent across the night sky! I'm sure you too would have fallen on your knees in fright and "wonder at the sight."

But Jesus did not remain a baby in a manger. "Through all his days," starting with his childhood and teen years, he "pleased his Father," obeyed and honored his parents. In fact, he "through all his days the Law obeyed." Jesus not only came to die in our place on the cross, fully to pay the curse of the Law; he also came to fulfill the Law, to obey his Father's will perfectly, and to impute (to ascribe or credit) his righteousness to the account of his sheep, of all who believe in him.

In the next two stanzas, we follow Jesus into the Garden of Gethsemane, where he shed "drops of grief" and wrestled in anguished prayer through the night, then suffered the ignominy of his betrayal, trial, beating, and crucifixion "for transgressions not his own." But that was not the end! He rose from the dead and "took death's sting away!" And, what's more, he made his conquest of death and judgment for his children, for all those to whom he gives "life and light," eternal life.

Then, wonder of wonders, Jesus, who laid aside his splendor when he came as a baby in Bethlehem, will once again in his Second Coming be heralded by angels as "Triumphant Jesus, King of kings!" when he comes again, this time in glorious splendor!

What will your response be? Like the shepherds, we'll fall on our knees; if you belong to Jesus, then you will rise joyfully to your feet, open your mouth, and "Eternal praise we'll shout to him." What should your response be today?

**For discussion**

1. What are some of the differences between this carol and others in this devotional?
2. For every poem that gets sung by Christians, hundreds, maybe even thousands, of years after it was written, there are likely far more

poems written that just aren't very singable. Discuss together as a family what makes you want to sing a particular carol.

3. I was long very reluctant to write a carol (or any hymn for that matter). Discuss what you think are strengths and weaknesses of "What wonder filled the starry night." You can listen to the music my friend and composer Greg Wilbur has written and recorded for this carol—and you can sing along at bondbooks.net/hymns.
4. Imagine yourself with the shepherds on that Judean hillside above Bethlehem, more than 2,000 years ago. What would you have done?
5. Read Mark 14:32-42 (and its parallels in the other Gospels). Imagine Jesus' anguish in the garden, sweating blood, his disciples sleeping, Jesus crying out to his Father, who would soon forsake him as he bears the sin of his children on the cross. Does it help you appreciate Jesus' Advent more to think about what he came to do?
6. What should be your response to all that Jesus came to do at Advent?

**Angels, from the Realms of Glory**

James Montgomery (1771-1854)

(December 13)

Angels, from the realms of glory,
Wing your flight o'er all the earth;
Ye who sang creation's story,
Now proclaim Messiah's birth:

Refrain:
Come and worship,
Come and worship,
Worship Christ, the newborn King.

Shepherds, in the fields abiding,
Watching o'er your flocks by night,
God with man is now residing,
Yonder shines the infant light:

Sages, leave your contemplations,
Brighter visions beam afar;

Seek the great Desire of nations,
Ye have seen his natal star:

Saints before the altar bending,
Watching long in hope and fear,
Suddenly the Lord, descending,
In his temple shall appear.

All creation, join in praising
God the Father, Spirit, Son;
Evermore your voices raising,
To th'eternal Three in One:

Refrain:
Come and worship,
Come and worship,
Worship Christ, the newborn King.

**About the poet**

Imagine someone writing a Christmas carol while locked up in a frigid prison cell? Poet and hymn writer James Montogomery, when he was a boy, was a missionary kid, his parents serving in the West Indies in a day when it was thought best for missionaries to leave their children back home in a boarding school. His parents both died within a year. Orphaned and alone in a Moravian boarding school, Montgomery turned to writing poetry. The Moravian influence drew him to writing hymn poetry, to be sung in worship.

Unable to finish his schooling, Montgomery attempted a literary life in London; he almost starved to death. For a time, he found temporary employment (and some free food) working in a bakery, and later in a book shop. Finally in Sheffield he was hired to work for the owner of the local newspaper. These were days of political conflict in England and abroad, and that conflict soon came to Montgomery's own door. His boss had to flee the country or be thrown in prison for running afoul of the government, and Montgomery was left to run the local newspaper.

Musing fondly on the West Indies where his parents had died, but where slave labor was used to produce sugar, soon brought the evils of the slave trade to his heart—and to his pen. Along with many others, Montgomery gave up eating sugar in protest of the evil trade, and even wrote articles in the newspaper critical of the government. Imagine his fear when the constable pounded on his door, arrested and tried him, and threw him in jail at York Castle—twice over. Undaunted, he used his time in jail for good purpose, writing more poetry, later published as *Prison Amusements* (1797). Though he had little formal literary training, he read and imitated the best poets and hymn writers, and soon gained public recognition for his many fine collections of poetry.

One of his finest hymns, a call to worship, expresses perfectly the Christian's attitude toward God in church—or in family or private devotions. Set to the rousing tune *Carlisle*, Montgomery's poetry compels you to stand when you sing it!

Stand up and bless the Lord,
You people of his choice;
Stand up, and bless the Lord your God
With heart and soul and voice.

After his death, the inhabitants of his beloved Sheffield commissioned a statue of him and had it set up in front of the cathedral, adding a stained-glass window to his memory inside. The inscription on his memorial reads: "Here lies interred, beloved by all who knew him, the Christian poet, patriot, and philanthropist. Wherever poetry is read, or Christian hymns sung, in the English language, 'he being dead, yet speaketh' by the genius, piety, and taste embodied in his writings."

Ranked by hymnologists alongside Charles Wesley and Isaac Watts, Montgomery cared most about writing hymns in praise of God, more than 400 of them—and at least one carol, "Angels, from the Realms of Glory."

**Looking more closely**

In the opening stanza of the carol, Montgomery explores the theme of the angels coming to "proclaim Messiah's birth:" The poet imagines angels singing the grand story of God creating the world out of nothing in six days, and now proclaiming his birth in song. He concludes each stanza with the repeated call to "Come and worship… Christ, the newborn King."

Then in the second stanza, the poet imagines the angels calling the shepherds to "Come and worship," declaring that "God with man is now residing," and pointing them to go to the stable in Bethlehem where Jesus the Light of the world was born.

Next, Montgomery shifts our vantage point to angels that he imagines encountered the "Sages," another name for wisemen. The angels tell them to leave off their "contemplations," all the deep things wisemen talk about and study. But why leave off these things?

"Brighter visions beam afar"; what you are about to see is greater than anything else you can know, and the angels urge them to follow the "natal star," natal meaning birth, which is where we get the name for a nativity scene.

Then the poet encapsulates millennia of redemptive anticipation. Everything in the Old Testament, blood sacrifices of animals on the altar, the saints of old, the prophets, the faithful believers, "Watching long in hope and fear." When will he come? When will he descend, God with us, and appear in his holy temple to redeem us? The angels are crying—he's here! "Come and worship… Christ, the newborn King."

Beside himself with joy, Montgomery, in a grand finale, has the angels now call "All creation" to join in the majestic song to the Trinity, "God the Father, Spirit, Son." Our poet is ecstatic and wants to share this stupendously Good News—with the whole world! Montgomery wants everyone to join in worshiping the Triune God, "the eternal Three in One," and to do so without ceasing: "Evermore your voices raise!"

**For discussion**

1. In the third stanza, Montgomery wrote, "Seek the great Desire of nations," and Charles Wesley wrote a carol with a stanza that begins: "Come, Desire of nations, come." To discover where this expression comes from, we have to go back to the clean pages in our Bibles; look up and read together Haggai 2:7. What do you think "Desire of nations" means?

2. Montgomery actually wrote two more stanzas to this carol. Why do you think this stanza isn't included in most hymnals?

   Sinners, wrung with true repentance,
   Doomed for guilt to endless pains,
   Justice now revokes the sentence,
   Mercy calls you—break your chains:

3. In yet another stanza almost always omitted, Montgomery refers to the judgment day when every knee will bow before Christ the King. Read and discuss Philippians 2:10-11. What does it mean that every knee will bow? Does it mean everyone eventually will be saved?
4. What does it mean for you to bow your knee to Jesus today and "Come and worship… Christ the newborn King"?

**All Praise to Thee, Eternal Lord**

Martin Luther (1483-1546)

(December 14)

All praise to thee, Eternal Lord,
Clothed in a garb of flesh and blood;
Choosing a manger for thy throne,
While worlds on worlds are thine alone.

Once did the skies before thee bow;
A virgin's arms contain thee now,
While angels, who in thee rejoice,
Now listen for thine infant voice.

A little Child, thou art our guest,
That weary ones in thee may rest;
Forlorn and lowly is thy birth;
That we may rise to heaven from earth.

Thou comest in the darksome night

To make us children of the light;
To make us, in the realms divine,
Like thine own angels round thee shine.

All this for us thy love hath done;
By this to thee our love is won;
For this we tune our cheerful lays,
And sing our thanks in ceaseless praise.

**About the poet**

Every once in a while, in history, God raises up giants in the land, extraordinary individuals called upon to do mighty deeds against vicious enemies, and equipped by God's grace to make a lasting impact for the gospel and Kingdom of God. Martin Luther was one of these men. Born the son of a Saxon miner in 1483, Luther would grow up to contend with popes and cardinals, dukes and monarchs, even an emperor.

One day, deeply troubled about his sins, a violent storm arose, and Luther was nearly struck by lightning. Terrified, he fell to the ground and promised that if God spared him, he would become a monk. Though he was scrupulous in doing all the good works he could, he found no peace with God in the monastery. "If ever a monk got to heaven by his monkery, it was I." But however much he worked and tried to win God's favor, it was never enough.

Finally, while studying the Bible, he came to see that he could never be justified before God by his good works; even his good works were filthy rags compared to God's holiness. One day he read, "The just shall live by faith" (Romans 1:17); it all made sense. God justified sinners by his grace, and gives them the gift of faith; this saving faith produces good works, but no one is justified by their good works. Suddenly it was as if the gates of paradise opened to him, and he was wonderfully justified. From then on, Luther was a man on fire, proclaiming everywhere that the Bible alone teaches that we are justified by grace alone, through faith alone, in Christ alone, to the glory of God alone.

But the Roman Catholic Church had made it illegal to proclaim this Good News. Believing he would be condemned and burned at the stake, Luther was stalwart; he even declared before the most powerful emperor in Europe that he would preach the Bible alone, regardless of the cost. "Here I stand," he said, "God help me; I can do no otherwise."

Though he was under the sentence of execution, and many wanted him dead, Luther never stopped. He preached. He debated. He wrote so many books he became the most published author in the 16th-century. He translated the Bible into German so that common people could hear God speak to them in his Word. And he wrote hymns in German so that God's people could respond in praise and adoration to Christ in their worship.

Giant that he was, you might think Luther was too busy for children, but you would be wrong. Some of his hymns were written specifically for children, and eventually, Luther himself would marry an apostate nun named Katharina von Bora, and they would have a number of their own children. Made fun of by some of his neighbors, Luther even helped with the diapers! "Let them laugh," murmured Luther through the clothes pins. "God and the angels smile in heaven."

Luther wanted to reform false teaching in the church, and he wanted to reform false worship in the church, but he also wanted to reform Christian marriage and the family according to the Bible. After writing a treatise on marriage, Luther composed "All praise to thee, Eternal Lord." A carol all about the Christ child, Luther wrote it specifically for children to sing—his own children! Imagine Luther and his wife Katie and their ten children singing together in their family worship!

**Luther on the role of music**

Luther grew up during the Renaissance, or rebirth, of cultural things like art, poetry, and music. It was expected that an educated person would develop skill in poetry and music—and Luther did! "Next to the Word of God," he wrote, "music deserves the highest praise. She is a mistress and governess of those human emotions... which control men or more often overwhelm them... Whether you wish to comfort the sad, to subdue frivolity, to encourage the despairing, to humble the proud, to calm the passionate, or to appease those full of hate... what more effective means could you find than music?"

Luther practiced what he preached. He played the lute, a stringed instrument that looks like a pear-shaped guitar, and he wrote a number of hymns; at least two of them were Christmas carols.

Though Luther did compose music for his hymns, including the tune for his most famous hymn "A Mighty Fortress," called the battle hymn of the Protestant Reformation, the music for "All Praise to Thee, Eternal Lord" was composed by another German from Saxony named Robert Schumann. Schumann's father, like Luther's, wanted him to become a lawyer, but he preferred playing the piano and composing music instead of studying law. He probably wouldn't have made a very good lawyer. But he would go on to be one of the greatest musical composers.

While studying piano with a master teacher, Schumann first met Clara, his teacher's nine-year-old daughter and piano prodigy. Schumann was smitten with the girl's piano playing, and the remarkable story of her trauma-induced deafness; when she was five, her mother had committed adultery and abandoned Clara and her siblings. In the intervening years, she had been raised by her father, who's nurture and piano instruction had restored her hearing—and had set free her musical gift. As the years passed, Schumann became smitten with the young woman herself. It took years before he finally persuaded her protective father to let him marry Clara!

Schumann's best-loved works were the many piano compositions he wrote especially to be played by his beloved and skillful wife Clara. *Canonbury* he composed in 1839, almost 300 years after Luther's death. Once it was arranged to accompany Luther's carol, it was a poetic and musical marriage made in heaven.

**Looking more closely**

There is a beautiful simplicity in Luther's poetry, as if he wanted to captivate the mind, imagination, and heart of a child—which is exactly what he wanted! Notice that each stanza is written in direct address as a sung prayer to Jesus the "Eternal Lord."

Luther wants us to be in awe at the irony of God choosing a lowly feeding trough for cattle in which to be born "While worlds on worlds are thine alone"; ironies like these make us amazed. In fact, each stanza features a situational irony, contrasting realities that don't at first seem like they should go together. The earth, the sky, the sea and everything in them all bow down to Jesus their Creator—but here he is a little baby contained and enfolded in Mary's arms. How can it be? Imagine with Luther the hosts of angels straining to hear the first sounds of Jesus' infant cooing like any other baby would do.

Then in stanza three, Luther wants us to contemplate the littleness of the child, of the baby, but in whom "weary ones in thee may rest." And wonder of wonders, Jesus' low and humble birth, his coming from heaven to earth, was for the saving purpose "That we may rise to heaven from earth."

Continuing the ironies in stanza four, Luther contrasts the darkness of the night in which Jesus was born with his purpose in coming, "To make us children of the light." What irony! And further, to make us shine like the angels that encircle the Savior with unending praises "in the realms divine."

In the final stanza, Luther ends where he began. In poetry that's called an inclusio. "We love him because he first loved us." And what else can we do for such a loving Savior? We tune our voices, and offer cheerful songs, "and sing our thanks in ceaseless praise." The Good News is too wonderful! We just can't stop singing "All praise to thee, Eternal Lord"!

**For discussion**

1. Luther used to think that he had to love God, do good works, win God's favor—and then if he did all that God would love him in return. Read I John 4:19 and discuss how Luther expressed these words in the carol and what this truth means.
2. List and discuss some of the ironies in this carol (remember, ironies are things that seem like opposites, things that contrast with each other and don't seem to go together).
3. What is a poetic inclusio? And give an example of how Luther uses the inclusio in this carol.
4. Though Luther wrote this carol before he had any children of his own, once he and Katie had children, they had daily family worship; there's even paintings of Luther accompanying his family's singing with his lute. Do you think the Luthers sang this carol together at Christmas? Shall we join them?

**Brightest and Best of the Sons of the Morning**

Reginald Heber (1783-1826)

(December 15)

Brightest and best of the sons of the morning,
Dawn on our darkness and lend us thine aid;
Star of the East, the horizon adorning,
Guide where our infant Redeemer is laid.

Cold on his cradle the dewdrops are shining;
Low lies his head with the beasts of the stall;
Angels adore him in slumber reclining,
Maker and Monarch and Savior of all!

Say, shall we yield him, in costly devotion,
Odors of Edom and off'rings divine?
Gems of the mountain and pearls of the ocean,
Myrrh from the forest, or gold from the mine?

Vainly we offer each ample oblation,
Vainly with gifts would his favor secure;
Richer by far is the heart's adoration,
Dearer to God are the prayers of the poor.

Brightest and best of the sons of the morning,
Dawn on our darkness and lend us thine aid;
Star of the East, the horizon adorning,
Guide where our infant Redeemer is laid.

**About the poet**

Reginald Heber was born the same year the American War for Independence ended in 1783. He began his life in a Christian family, where his parents' godly nurture began blossoming early in his life. As a five-years-old, when someone recited a passage of Scripture, Reginald could give the chapter and verse! When he was seven, he was writing poetry, some of it he translated first from Latin. He took the Bible's message about being kind toward the poor so seriously that his mother had to sew his spending money into his pockets so he wouldn't give it all away!

While some of Heber's classmates excelled at rugby, during his university years at Brasenose College, Oxford, Heber excelled at poetry. Under the literary influence of the family friend and famous poet and novelist, Sir Walter Scott, Heber won two distinguished prizes for poetry, and another for an English prose essay. He was a rising star among English Romantic poets.

In 1807, Heber took up his ministerial duties as pastor in the village of Hodnet near the Welsh border. Following in his father's footsteps, Heber believed one of his important tasks was to improve the sung worship of the country folks in his parish. The *Olney Hymns* of William Cowper and John Newton were not widely available, so Heber set to work writing his own hymnal. The bishop of London, however, refused to allow its publication; Anglicans still only permitted the singing of strict Psalm versifications in church.

In 1809, Heber fell in love with a pastor's daughter from the parish church in Wrexham, Wales. On a nearby stone wall, there's a plaque that celebrates Heber's courtship and marriage to the pastor's daughter, Amelia. In 1818, Amelia gave birth to their first daughter, but a few months later, to their grief, their infant daughter died—on Christmas Eve. God later gave them two more daughters.

Displayed in a window of the medieval church in Wrexham is the original hand-written manuscript of Heber's hymn about Christian missions, "From Greenland's Icy Mountains." It's a hymn about the doctrine of total depravity, and the need all people have of the saving grace of God in Christ; in the hymn, Heber used the word "vile" to refer to all of us as sinners, and he called those who didn't believe in Christ "heathens." Heber wanted all people of every ethnicity to know the Good News of the saving grace of Jesus found only in the Christian gospel, but first they had to know the bad news. Jesus came to seek and to save sinners, and only sinners can know the saving grace of the gospel.

Later, Ghandi, the leader of India, publicly denounced the hymn. He didn't believe that all people are sinners and that the Christian gospel is the only way of salvation. But Heber was passionate about everybody, including East Indians, knowing the gospel of Jesus

Christ, who alone is the Way, the Truth, and the Life for all people—including the heathen.

During his years in Hodnet, Heber preached tirelessly in support of foreign missions, and the spread of the gospel throughout the world by evangelism. In 1823, an opportunity arose for him to engage personally in that work. He was called to be the Anglican bishop of Calcutta; he went from pastoring a little country village church, to pastoring a parish that consisted of almost the entire sub-continent of India! In a country with an institutionalized caste system of prejudice against the low-born and poor, Heber was a vigorous advocate for the equitable treatment of all people: male or female, rich or poor, slave or free. For him, this was an essential part of spreading the gospel of Jesus Christ to all people throughout India.

One swelteringly hot East-Indian day in 1826, Heber preached to a large crowd in the open air, the sun beating down on his brow. After his sermon, though otherwise healthy, he suffered a stroke and died. Imagine Amelia Heber's grief, and that of their two living daughters. So well-known and loved was Heber, that Christians throughout England and Indian mourned his loss.

Along with "Brightest and Best," two other Heber hymns are still sung in churches that sing hymns. "The Son of God Goes Forth to War," is a vigorous anthem, celebrating the faithful martyrs who have gone before us, and calling all Christians, "men and boys, the matron and the maid," to "follow in their train," in their footsteps as they followed the Lord Jesus to suffering and death.

Even better known and loved is Heber's, "Holy, Holy, Holy," a hymn rich with appropriate language extoling the nature of the Triune God. Heber overwhelms our imaginations with majestic adoration of the thrice-holy God: Father, Son, and Holy Spirit. I particularly love the image of all the saints adoring the Lord in heaven, "casting down their golden crowns" at the feet of Christ the Redeemer.

We wouldn't even have heard of this carol written by Reginald Heber if it weren't for his beloved wife Amelia. A year after her husband died, Amelia had gathered all of his hymns together and had them published in 1827; from there, his best-loved hymns made their way into hymnals across all denominational lines.

**A word about tunes**

Unlike many Christmas carols, Heber's "Brightest and Best of the Sons of the Morning," does not have a single tune attached to it. The g-minor tune *Star in the East*, an American Southern Harmony melody, variously arranged and attributed, as far as I'm concerned, is the best tune most suited to sustain the weight and grandeur of the themes Heber explores in his fine Advent poetry.

**Looking more closely**

In 1811, Heber borrowed a little school composition book from one of his daughters, dipped his quill in ink, and set down the five stanzas of "Brightest and Best of the Sons of the Morning," another carol that tells a story. And what a story to tell—full of wonder and mystery!

In Matthew's Gospel we learn about wisemen from the east who followed a special star to Bethlehem. Were these pagan astrologists who believed that they could gain wisdom from worshipping the stars? I doubt it. It makes far more sense that the wisemen were descendants of exiled Jews who had for centuries been living in captivity in the east—in modern day Iraq and Iran. And these wise men were also patient men; their people had for generations been waiting, watching, longing for the coming of the promised Messiah. God has promised that there will always be "a remnant, chosen by grace" (Romans 11:5). Likely the wisemen were some of that remnant.

Heber's carol begins contemplating the star that appeared in the east, "the horizon adorning." And then the persona in the poem, as if he were one of the wisemen, implores the star to "Guide where our infant Redeemer is laid."

And where is the infant Redeemer laid? In a cradle, but not an ordinary cradle; Jesus "in slumber reclining," is in a feeding trough, his head lies so lowly, "with the beasts of the stall"! Can you picture the scene as Heber paints it for us? Jesus is lying in a livestock stable, with no central heating, and subject to the night's cold dewy drops forming on his swaddling bands and the manger where he lies. Meanwhile, "Angels adore him" where he slumbers, and what is the substance of their adoration? This lowly, humble-born infant, is "Maker and Monarch, and Savior of all!"

If he really is all those things, Heber continues in stanza three, what kind of gift can we bring to such an exalted one as he? Surely if he is God the Creator, King of kings, Savior of sinners, and the wisemen are going to properly adore him, theirs will be "costly devotion." Maybe they should bring expensive perfume from the east, or "Gems of the mountains and pearls of the ocean,/Myrrh from the forest, or gold from the mine?" In other words, if Jesus is all these grand and glorious things, Lord of all, we need to find the best, the finest, the costliest gifts to bring him—gold, frankincense, and myrrh might do. He is worthy of nothing less.

Do you see the pathway of thought and imagination on which Heber is taking us? In stanza four, he declares all those costly gifts to be vanity of vanities, that is, empty, unworthy oblations; however ample, full and lavish the gifts we pour out to him, none of these things that our hands can bring to him "would his favor secure." No, God prefers our hearts to the rich gifts from our hands; he wants us to see how poor in spirit we really are, that there is nothing good in us that we can bring that will secure God's good favor. The only way to find favor with a holy God is to acknowledge that we are not rich in ourselves; we have nothing; we are poor, penniless. God desires "the prayers of the poor," the prayer of the cheating tax collector in Jesus' parable, the prayer of one who knows his poverty, "God, be merciful to me the sinner."

When we come empty-handed, "nothing in our hands we bring," to the "Maker and Monarch and Savior," with our sin and poverty alone, to "the infant Redeemer," to the one who came "to save his people from their sins," then and only then do we have peace, rest, and salvation forevermore!

**For discussion**

1. Read and discuss Matthew 2:1-12, the account of the wisemen following the star to Bethlehem.

2. Though the biblical account doesn't say how many, why do people think there were only three wisemen? Can you think of a carol that celebrates there being only three wisemen from the east, or from the orient?
3. What were the two words that made one of Heber's hymns so unpopular? What do we need to know first before we can know and believe the Good News of the gospel.
4. What were some of the ways God prepared and equipped Heber to write such a wonderful carol (and other hymns)?
5. Though Heber wrote this carol in 1811, can you find any phrases he might have recalled in his grieving at the death of his infant daughter on Christmas Eve in 1818? Losing a child to premature death is always a great grief to parents and siblings, but why might losing a baby so near Christmas be an even harder providence?
6. Though we can't earn salvation by giving God expensive gifts, or doing good works, yet in gratitude for the "indescribable gift" of Jesus himself, what gifts ought you to give to him today—and throughout every day of your life until we see Jesus face-to-face for evermore?

**As with Gladness Men of Old**

William Chatterton Dix (1837-1865)

(December 16)

As with gladness men of old
Did the guiding star behold;
As with joy they hailed its light,
Leading onward, beaming bright;
So, most gracious God, may we
Evermore be led to thee.

As with joyful steps they sped
To that lowly cradle-bed,
There to bend the knee before
Him whom heav'n and earth adore;
So may we with willing feet
Ever seek thy mercy-seat.

As they offered gifts most rare
At that cradle rude and bare;
So may we with holy joy,

Pure, and free from sin's alloy,
All our costliest treasures bring,
Christ, to thee, our heav'nly King.

Holy Jesus, every day
Keep us in the narrow way;
And, when earthly things are past,
Bring our ransomed souls at last
Where they need no star to guide,
Where no clouds thy glory hide.

In that heav'nly country bright
Need they no created light;
Thou its Light, its Joy, its Crown,
Thou its Sun which goes not down;
There forever may we sing
Alleluias to our King.

Do you remember learning about poet William Chatterton Dix, born near the Welsh border, who spent much of his life in Scotland working for a maritime insurance company? He was brought to faith in Christ, you will remember, when in 1865 he came down with a severe illness that nearly took his life.

During Dix's slow recovery, plagued with fear and deep depression, gospel light broke through the gloom and he was transformed by the saving power of God. The key to his spiritual awakening was his serious reading and studying of the Bible. His way of meditating on the Word, was by writing poetry about what he read. Dix was equipped to write hymns and carols because the aesthetic skill needed to do so was already in place. Remember, educated people in his day generally had much more early training in literature, poetry, music, and theology than in our day.

Along with his carol "What Child is this?" and others, Mr. Dix's "As with Gladness" was first published in 1871 in a celebrated collection entitled, "*Christmas Carols, Old and New*."

**Looking more closely**

The poet organized each six-line stanza (sestet) in three rhyming couplets, the first four lines describing some dimension of the wisemen's encounter with the star and with the Christ child, then ending the sestet with two lines of application.

For example, in the opening stanza, Dix describes the "men of old" full of gladness at the appearance of the "guiding star." They responded with joy and hailed its light, pointing the way, "Leading onward, beaming bright." The poet then shifts to what our response ought to be as we sing the carol. By God's grace, we ought "Evermore [to] be led to thee." Far from chafing at and begrudging God's will, just as the wisemen were filled with joy at God's guidance, so ought we to embrace his will and way with gladness.

The wisemen in the second stanza, turn their "joyous steps" with speed to follow the star to the "lowly cradle-bed." I used to tell my six children when they were young, "Delayed obedience is disobedience." The wisemen understood this; they made haste. When God made the way to Jesus clear to them with his star shining in the east, they moved fast. No distraction, no procrastination, no side roads or byways—nothing could come between them and following the way to their Savior.

And what did the wisemen do when they came to Jesus' "lowly cradle-bed"? They fell to their knees in adoration of Jesus as God the Son. Dix wants us to do the same: "So may we with willing feet/Ever seek they mercy seat." God only wants cheerful worshipers, ones with "willing feet." He wants no one to come to him kicking the gravel, casting about, scowling left and right—wishing there was some other pathway.

Seeking God's mercy-seat is another way of calling us to worship and prayer. In mercy, God does not give us what we deserve, eternal punishment for our sin and rebellion against his law. That's what we deserve, each one of us. The mercy-seat is where we meet with God, where he hears our cries, where he extends his loving mercy upon us.

In the third stanza, the wisemen "offered gifts most rare/At the cradle, rude and bare," likely referring to the "rude and bare" feeding trough into which Mary laid Jesus after she gave birth. But did the wisemen come to the stable and offer their gifts to an infant Jesus, lying in a manger? Take a look at your nativity scene. It likely includes the wisemen at the stable, alongside the shepherds.

There's been a long tradition of conflating the adoration of the shepherds and the wisemen into the same episode, the night of Jesus' birth. The Bible is clear that the shepherds came the night Jesus was born, but it's equally clear that the wisemen came a while later, and the star that guided them came to rest over the "house" where the child lay (Matt. 2:1-12), not the stable; likely the wisemen's visit came many months, maybe even up to two years after Jesus' birth. Jesus would have been a toddler not an infant lying in a "cradle, rude and bare"!

Recall that Herod, after he heard the news from the wisemen, in his zeal to destroy a rival king, had all the infant males two years old or younger murdered; at least evil Herod and his star-gazing chronologists thought Jesus' birth could have been as much as two years earlier.

But the application the poet wants us to make is to be like the wisemen; join with the generous, gift-giving travelers from the east. We are urged, "with holy joy," to bring "our costliest treasures" to "Christ… our heavenly King."

In the fourth stanza, the poet turns to prayer, and makes an appeal for "Holy Jesus" to "Keep us in the narrow way." And then he prays that Jesus would "Bring our ransomed souls at last," to be with him in heaven, where there will no longer be the need for a star to guide us, and where Christ's glory will never more be shrouded in clouds. Bring us at last to heaven, is a prayer Jesus delights to answer for all his children. What Jesus starts in salvation, he always finishes.

The final stanza gives us a window into "that heavenly country bright," where there will be no sun or moon, because Jesus will be heaven's "Light, its Joy, its Crown/Thou its Sun which goes not down." And what will we be doing in such a glorious place? "There forever may we sing/Alleluias to our King." We can start doing that right now!

**For discussion**

1. Read Matthew 2:1-12, and discuss the account of the wisemen coming to worship Jesus.
2. Based on your reading of Matthew's account, do you think the wisemen were there with the shepherds the night of Jesus' birth? Why or why not?
3. How many wisemen are there in your nativity scene? Does the biblical account tell us how many? There's a carol that begins, "We three kings of Orient are…" What do you think is the basis for there being three wisemen, even though the biblical account doesn't say how many there were? (Hint: how many gifts are mentioned?).
4. People who worship idols bring gifts of food and other things to their gods. Do we need to bring costly gifts to Jesus in order for him to love us and save us?
5. Read Luke 20:25 and discuss what Jesus means when he tells us to give to God what is God's. Though you cannot manipulate God by bringing him gifts, what does God require of you in your life as a Christian? What should you be giving to God today?

**Thou Who Wast Rich Beyond All Splendor**

Frank Houghton (1894-1972)

(December 17)

Thou who wast rich beyond all splendor,
All for love's sake becamest poor;
Thrones for a manger didst surrender,
Sapphire-paved courts for stable floor.
Thou who wast rich beyond all splendor,
All for love's sake becomes poor.

Thou who art God beyond all praising,
All for love's sake becamest man;
Stooping so low, but sinners raising
Heavenwards by thine eternal plan.
Thou who art God beyond all praising,
All for love's sake becamest man.

Thou who art love beyond all telling,

Savior and King, we worship thee.
Emmanuel, within us dwelling,
Make us what thou wouldst have us be.
Thou who art love beyond all telling,
Savior and King, we worship thee.

**A missionary poet**

Born in 1894, Frank Houghton became an Anglican minister who, like Reginald Heber before him, was deeply committed to the Great Commission and to taking the gospel to faraway lands. His wife Dorothy was the daughter of one of the "Cambridge Seven," as they were called, seven young men studying at the university who together believed that God had called them to the work of the gospel in overseas missions. In 1920, Houghton became a missionary with the China Inland Mission, founded by Hudson Taylor, and would later become the director general of the mission board. He met and married Dorothy Cassels in 1923 in China where she had grown up as the daughter of a missionary.

Houghton was known as a missionary bishop, poet, and author of several books on missions, including one about missionary to India Amy Carmichael. One of the missionary hymns Houghton wrote, "Facing a Task Unfinished," Keith Getty said, "is the best hymn about missions ever written." Houghton wrote it in the 1930s in an effort to recruit 200 more missionaries for the work in China. Krysten Getty has written a new refrain for the hymn, and the Gettys have set it to new music, in hopes that it might be used of God to call many to the work of the gospel around the world.

When Houghton came to China in 1920, there were only a few hundred thousand Christians in the entire vast country of 400,000 million people. With more than a billion people today, there are more than 80 million Christians in China; that may be more Christians than in any other country on the planet. Houghton's gospel work contributed to that expansion, and his hymn writing likely played no small part in that growth.

**Looking more closely**

In his opening line, Houghton makes an allusion to what the Apostle Paul wrote, "For you know the grace of our Lord Jesus Christ, that though he was rich, yet for our sake he became poor, so that we through his poverty might become rich" (2 Corinthians 8:9). And why did Jesus do it? "All for love's sake," the poet tells us. In the middle two lines of the stanza, we're shown the vast contrast of the glorious splendor of heaven that Jesus left behind to come into the world, to lay aside his glory and become the God-man, born in a rustic stable and laid in a livestock feeding trough, bejeweled courts and thrones left behind. Jesus willingly became poor so that we his children might become rich beyond measure, and he did it "All for love's sake."

In the second stanza, Houghton directly addresses the Lord Jesus "who [is] God beyond all praising," and who became a man, "All for love's sake." And it was all by the eternal plan of Father, Son, and Holy Spirit, the covenant of redemption, that in order to raise sinners heavenward, Jesus would willingly have to stoop so low.

And the poet reminds us again that Jesus, the baby in the manger, is fully God and worthy of all praising.

What are we to do with such a message? What is the only response we can render to him who himself is "love beyond all telling"? "Savior and King, we worship thee." He gave up everything, all his riches, made himself poor, in order to make we poor sinners rich for all eternity. Now, with God himself dwelling within us, the poet prays that Emmanuel would "Make us what thou wouldst have us be." And we are left to ponder, what would God have us to be?

At creation, man was made to worship God; by the gospel, we have been remade to worship him in newness of life by the substitution of Jesus, him taking our place, becoming poor, in our place, and giving us his place, "who was rich beyond on splendor." If he is our "Savior and King," we want to worship him. We want to serve him. We want to please and obey him, to delight in his will and way. We don't want to do anything that displeases him. His great love for us makes us want everything we think, and say, and do, to bring him praise and glory and honor.

Commenting on the poet's objective, Keith Getty said, "Frank Houghton understood that what we sing affects what we think, how we feel, what we pray for, and, ultimately, every decision we make in life." If that's true, and I believe it is, we should be very careful what we sing, don't you think?

**For discussion**

1. Reread 2 Corinthians 8:9 and discuss the biblical source for this carol. What parallels do you see

between the biblical text and the words of the carol?

2. The opening line of each stanza ends with the phrase "beyond all splendor," "beyond all praising," and "beyond all telling." Discuss the effect of the poet using the words "beyond all" before each of the ending words of the first line of each stanza?
3. Reread I John 4:19 and discuss together what ought to motivate all of our worship and obedience to God?
4. If a wealthy king made you his heir and gave you all the riches of his kingdom, how would you want to show your gratitude? What are ways you can show your love to King Jesus for laying aside the splendor of his heavenly kingdom and riches and becoming poor so that you might become rich?
5. Why is it so important to choose carefully what we sing?

**All My Heart This Night Rejoices**

Paul Gerhardt (1607-1676)

Catherine Winkworth (1829-1878)

(December 18)

All my heart this night rejoices,
As I hear, far and near,
Sweetest angel voices;
"Christ is born," their choirs are singing,
Till the air, everywhere,
Now their joy is ringing.

Forth today the Conqueror goeth,
Who the foe, sin and woe,
Death and hell, o'erthroweth.
God is man, man to deliver;
His dear Son now is one
With our blood forever.

Shall we still dread God's displeasure,
Who, to save, freely gave

His most cherished Treasure?
To redeem us, he hath given
His own Son from the throne
Of his might in heaven.

He becomes the Lamb that taketh
Sin away and for aye
Full atonement maketh.
For our life his own he tenders
And our race, by his grace,
Meet for glory renders.

Hark! A voice from yonder manger,
Soft and sweet, doth entreat,
"Flee from woe and danger;
Brethren, from all ills that grieve you,
You are freed; all you need
I will surely give you."

Come, then, banish all your sadness,
One and all, great and small;
Come with songs of gladness.
Love him who with love is glowing;
Hail the star, near and far
Light and joy bestowing.

Dearest Lord, thee will I cherish;
Though my breath fail in death,
Yet I shall not perish;
But with thee abide forever,
There on high, in that joy
Which can vanish never.

**About the poet**

Lover of music that he was, Martin Luther inspired many other German hymn writers. One of the most prolific was Paul Gerhardt, born over fifty years after Luther's death, the same year that Jamestown was founded in colonial America, in 1607. By sheer numbers of hymns still included in hymnals, Gerhardt went on to outwrite Luther four to one.

Following in Luther's giant footsteps, Gerhardt studied theology at the University of Wittenberg. After completing his studies, he had two dreams: to marry the young woman he loved and to pastor a Lutheran church. And then the Holy Roman Empire viciously attacked German Protestant towns and the grinding devastation of the Thirty Years' War began. Some historians estimate that from 1618 to 1648 more than a third of the population perished in the conflict.

Gerhardt worked as a private tutor in the home of a Berlin lawyer and kept his hopes alive by writing poetry. Not until he turned forty-eight years old and became an assistant minister in Berlin did he and his sweetheart, Anna Maria, finally marry.

God gave them four children—but they all died in infancy. Anna Maria gave birth to a fifth child—a boy. While the child lived and grew stronger, Gerhardt's precious wife grew weaker; she never recovered from childbirth, and, eventually, much to her husband's grief, she died; Gerhardt was a young widower with a toddler to care for. Meanwhile, in his ministry, differences between local pastors arose, and he finally lost his pulpit and congregation in Berlin. He finished out his years with his son in a small country parish, preaching faithfully to a largely unresponsive congregation. And yet he persisted in writing sacred poetry.

It was said of Gerhardt that he wrote his hymns "under circumstances that would have made most men cry rather than sing." Though beset by trials and afflictions, Gerhardt's humble devotion to Jesus fills his hymns. There's a fluid simplicity and a hearty sincerity to his poetry; his rich and honest lyrics resonated with worshipers in his own day; and today German Christians sing more Gerhardt hymns than any other.

Moravian Christians loved singing German hymns; John and Charles Wesley, while caught in a violent Atlantic storm were deeply moved by their singing—as the terrified Wesley brothers hung on for dear life, as the ship careened and plunged in the seas. Many of those hymns were written by Paul Gerhardt.

**About the English translator/poet**

Catherine Winkworth, born in 1829, contributed to the great literary accomplishments of many other Christians living in Victorian England. It is said that she was a person of remarkable intellectual and social gifts, especially distinguished for her combination of rare literary ability and vast knowledge, yet with a certain tender and sympathetic refinement. Her spiritual piety, adorned by poetic and foreign language skills, enabled her to become the most well-loved and faithful English translator of German hymns.

Recall how difficult it is to translate poetry from one language to another. English uses different words to express the same ideas, words that don't fit the sound and syllables used by Gerhardt to create the German rhyme scheme and meter in this carol. It takes near genius to convey all the original nuance of meaning while still keeping the poetry intact; not at all an easy task.

Catherine Winkworth deserves our admiration. We are deeply in her debt for giving us this wonderful carol (and many other German hymns) in English. After a fruitful life, she died in Switzerland in 1878. Buried in Geneva, she is appreciatively memorialized in Bristol Cathedral, near the Welsh border where she was born.

**Looking more closely**

German hymns were often passionate prayers, ones that reflect these earnest Christians' immediate relationship and constant conversation with the Lord Jesus. Even the structure of their poetic lines shows this.

Maybe with all the troubles Gerhardt suffered, he was less interested in creating longer more eloquent lines of poetry; his lyric sounds more like tormented crying out to the Lord in distress—as the Psalmists were so often doing. The short punctuated, rhyming lines give audible testimony to the agony of the poet's lament.

But there is considerable Job-like eloquence, a humble honesty, in his passionate plea to the Lord for deliverance and salvation. Gerhardt's short, punctuated lines help create a tone of utter dependence on the Lord, that there is no one else to help us; his faith expressed in these anguished lines is a genuine crying out to God for deliverance.

By the late sixteen-hundreds German hymns had taken on a more personal, devotional character. And increasingly, Jesus, the second person of the Godhead, was the object of that adoration. Maybe because Jesus had suffered so terribly for them, German Christians felt that he understood their suffering, and he alone could rescue them in their distress.

Though he suffered so much, Gerhardt's heart is overflowing with joy in this carol; he can hardly contain himself. He hears, and we with him, "Sweetest angel voices" filling the air with the joyful news that "Christ is born"!

In the second stanza, we learn more why Gerhardt is full of joy unspeakable, and yet he is speaking! The Conqueror, Jesus, has come to overthrow the powers of death and hell. God has stooped down; in the mystery of the incarnation, "God is man, man to deliver," and he is now one with our human blood. In what theologians call the hypostatic union, God has become man, fully God, and fully man, yet without sin, and to conquer sin, and death, and hell for all who believe in him.

In this third stanza, Gerhardt reasons with us, compels us to follow his line of thinking. "Shall we still dread God's displeasure"? How can it be? This marvelous God gave his "most cherished Treasure," his only Son to redeem us, and he is God on his throne, the Almighty One. Do you understand the wonder of what he is saying? When you place all your hope in Jesus, you never ever need to dread God's displeasure; and when you really get your mind and heart around what God has accomplished to save you, not only will you never dread his displeasure, but you will never want to do anything that brings him displeasure; you will want to bring him glory and honor, and trust, and heartfelt gratitude and obedience all your days.

Why? Because Jesus is the "Lamb that taketh/Sin away." As far as the east is from the west! He is the one who has made "Full atonement" for your sins; he is the one who gave his life for your life. What else can we render, can we give to him? By such a glorious grace, we render him all glory, laud, and honor.

In the next stanza, Gerhardt brilliantly takes us to the manger, to hear the voice of Jesus. Now, Jesus was a baby, a newborn, and newborn babies don't talk yet, do they? But Gerhardt is using a literary device, he's giving words to the infant Jesus that represent what he has come to accomplish. So, Jesus "speaks" and tells you to "Flee from woe and danger." You no longer need to be grieved at the ills, the troubles that surround you. "You are freed; all you need" Jesus "will surely give you." It is true. All that you need, Jesus will give to you.

Though Gerhardt suffered so much grief and woe, have you noticed the joy and gladness that fill his carol? In the next stanza, he calls us to "banish all [our] sadness," all of us, little ones, teenagers, moms and dads, grandmothers and grandfathers, "great and small/Come with songs of gladness." Gerhardt wants you to respond to Jesus' love with your love. He wants you this Advent season to "Hail the star" that pointed the way to Jesus, who came "Light and joy bestowing."

In the last magisterial stanza, Gerhardt shifts his view. He turns in prayer, in direct and resolved address: "Dearest Lord, thee will I cherish." We cherish the most important things. In your mother and father's marriage vows they said they would "love, honor, and cherish" one another all their days. I love the word cherish. God cherishes his Son; God cherishes his elect, those for whom his Son died. Yes, we will want more than anything in all the world to cherish God's Son too. And when we get sick or hurt, when it comes time to die, "Yet I shall not perish/But with thee abide forever."

How can a man who suffered so much, write poetry with such beauty, such faith, such trust, such firm grasp of the never-ending joy of eternity, "Which can vanish never"? Because Gerhardt knew that "Christ is born." That he came to deliver us. That he overthrew for all time "Death and hell." God is no longer displeased with us. Wonder of wonders, God cherishes us. We must cherish him too.

**For discussion**

1. Read together and discuss John 1:14. What does it mean that God the Word was made flesh? What does it mean to see God's glory? Do you see his glory?
2. Read together I John 3:1-3 and discuss what manner of love the Father has for his children. What does the unbelieving world think of those who are loved of God and who love him? What did the unbelieving world think of Jesus?
3. Reread together the final stanza of Gerhardt's magisterial carol. It is a prayer. Can you pray this prayer and really mean it with all your heart and soul?
4. Paul Gerhardt had many sadnesses in his life. What were some of them? How does God want you to respond when afflictions and sadness come into your life?

5. As a family, this Advent evening, join your hearts with joy together and with the angels, make the atmosphere in in your house ring with joy and gladness, because "Christ is born"!

**Angels We Have Heard on High**

Traditional French Carol

James Chadwick (1813-1882)

(December 19)

Angels we have heard on high,
Sweetly singing o'er the plains,
And the mountains in reply
Echoing their joyous strains:

Gloria, in excelsis Deo!
Gloria, in excelsis Deo!

Shepherds, why this jubilee?
Why your joyous strains prolong?
What the gladsome tidings be
Which inspire your heav'nly song?

*Gloria…*

Come to Bethlehem and see
Him whose birth the angels sing;

Come, adore on bended knee
Christ the Lord, the new-born King.

*Gloria…*

See him in a manger laid,
Jesus, Lord of heav'n and earth!
Mary, Joseph, lend your aid,
sing with us our Savior's birth.

*Gloria…*

**Glory to God**

"Angels We Have Heard on High" is one of the most compelling of our carols. We don't simply want to listen to the angels doing all the singing; we want to join with them singing "Glory to God in the highest"!

Do you ever wonder what the word "glory" means? Imagine "glory" being your final word on earth. When my father was in his teens, he went with his father to the deathbed of his grandfather, my great-grandfather, Charles Wesley Bond. He'd been unresponsive for days, just lying in a coma in his hospital bed in Gray's Harbor County, Washington. My father, a man not given to exaggeration, described seeing his unresponsive grandfather suddenly open his eyes; gazing in wonder at the ceiling, he lifted his hands heavenward, and in a hushed voice said, "Glory!" Then his hands dropped to his sides—and he died.

Sometimes people use "glory" as another name for heaven; it would appear that my great-grandfather was seeing a glimpse of the glories of heaven in the instant before his death. The angels said or sang to the shepherds, "*Glory* to God in the highest…" The Westminster Shorter Catechism begins with our chief end, our reason for being, "to *glorify* God and to enjoy him forever." Forms of the word pop up everywhere.

"Glory" is a multi-faceted word meaning, magnificence, honor, worship, praise—all the things of which God is so worthy, and that Christians want to render to the Triune God, Father, Son, and Holy Spirit. We were created for this purpose, for everything we are, and have, and do; with heart and hands and voices—to bring glory to God. And in doing so, we find our greatest enjoyment. Turning from our ridiculous attempts at self-glory, and giving glory to God is delightful to true Christians. And singing is one of the glorious ways we get to express our love and adoration to God.

The 18th-century French poet who originally wrote this carol is unknown, but Irish bishop James Chadwick freely versified and brought the carol into beautiful English poetry for us. Set to the infectious French folk melody *Gloria* (can you guess what that means in Latin?), it is a jubilant carol that leaves the congregation—or family—no other option than to sing from the heart and with full voice.

**Looking more closely**

The poet wants to shift our gaze to the point of view of the shepherds out on the hillsides, keeping watch over their flocks through the night. "Angels *we* have heard…" The "we" is the shepherds speaking, breathlessly recounting the angelic visitation they have just seen and heard. So thrilled are the shepherds in the carol, that they can't restrain themselves; they must join their voices with the angels, and with "the mountains in reply/Echoing their joyous strains."

In Christian history, the Latin refrain, "Gloria, in excelsis Deo," what the angel host sang in their announcement to the shepherds, is called the Greater Doxology; "Glory to God in the highest!" Fittingly, the poet ends each stanza by drawing us to sing with the angels, the mountains, and the shepherds.

In the second stanza, we are brought into the conversation and invited to ask the shepherds "why this jubilee?/Why your joyous strains prolong?" The shepherds could not contain themselves; they've joined the angels in the "gladsome tidings," their "heav'nly song." And by extension, we are compelled to sing along with them in the carol refrain, "Gloria in excelsis Deo!"

In the third stanza, the shepherds with evangelistic zeal invite us to "Come to Bethlehem and see" what all the angelic fuss is about. Down through the ages, Advent is a time to do just that, come to Bethlehem and see for ourselves, to see Jesus, the infant King about whom the angels sang.

Did the shepherds fully understand what was afoot? Mysteries still abound, but we are given much more understanding than they were. We have the New Testament, the Gospel accounts, the epistles with their in-depth theological explanations of redeeming love at work—all of which tells us much more of what was going on in a cattle shed in Judea 2,000 years ago.

How much more then today, as we "Come to Bethlehem and see," will we want not only to look at the new baby like the perplexed cattle were likely doing, but with fuller revelation, to see far beyond mere passive observation, and "adore on bended knee/Christ the Lord, the new-born King." And to give grateful substance to our adoration by singing "Glory to God in the highest!"

Singing is the only worthy response to such splendors: the angels, the mountains, the shepherds, and in the final stanza, because the infant is "Jesus, Lord of heaven and earth," it is only fitting that Jesus' parents join in the heavenly song; "Mary, Joseph, lend your aid," the poet calls, and render "Glory to God in the highest!"

What about you and me? Do you feel the pull? It is only fitting that we do the same. This is no time for yawning or for anemic murmuring! It is true that the incarnation is simply so splendid that the wonder of it all compels "all mortal flesh [to] keep silence." But something happens inside of us as the awe and reverence accelerates. There is a point in our worship when we can no longer keep silence. We cannot contain our joy. Along with the heavenly host, we are compelled to open wide our mouths and sing, with full voice and overflowing hearts, bursting at the seams with joy—and with *GLORY*!

**For discussion**

1. Why do you think that so many of our carols are written about the visitation of the angels to the shepherds?
2. Read together Luke 2:8-20. This carol is written from the point of view of the shepherds. What would you have been thinking and doing if you were a shepherd and suddenly the night sky was resplendent with angels?
3. What was my great-grandfather's last word on earth? All his neighbors called him "The Preacher," though he was never ordained as a preacher; he ran a hardware store, but throughout his lifetime he told everybody he met about Jesus. His final word was just an extension of what he was always talking about.
4. What would you like your last word to be? How can you be thinking, and speaking, and acting now so that the last words out of your mouth bring glory to God?

**See, Amid the Winter's Snow**

Edward Caswell (1814-1878)

John Goss (1800-1880)

(December 20)

See, amid the winter's snow,
Born for us on earth below,
See, the tender Lamb appears,
Promised from eternal years.

**Chorus**:
*Hail, thou ever blessed morn,*
*Hail redemption's happy dawn,*
*Sing through all Jerusalem,*
*Christ is born in Bethlehem.*

Lo, within a manger lies
He who built the starry skies;
He who, throned in height sublime,
Sits among the cherubim.
*Hail…*

Say, ye holy shepherds, say,
What your joyful news today;
Wherefore have ye left your sheep
On the lonely mountain steep?
*Hail…*

"As we watched at dead of night,
Lo, we saw a wondrous light:
Angels singing 'Peace on earth'
Told us of the Savior's birth."
*Hail…*

Sacred infant, all divine,
What a tender love was thine,
Thus to come from highest bliss
Down to such a world as this.
*Hail…*

Teach, O teach us, holy child,
By thy face so meek and mild,
Teach us to resemble thee,
In thy sweet humility.
*Hail…*

**In what season was Jesus born?**

"See, Amid the Winter's Snow" reminds us that Christmas has been celebrated on December 25, in the middle of winter, for many centuries. Many years ago (BC, before children), we spent a Christmas season bicycling all over New Zealand—in the middle of winter! Only, not winter weather in New Zealand or Australia, the countries "down under." We cycled in shorts and shirtsleeves. It was warm and sunny, at least a good bit of the two months we were there.

How do New Zealanders celebrate Christmas? They go to the beach and work on their tan! Though there's snow on Mt. Cook year around, there's no snow in the rest of the country at Christmas in the Southern Hemisphere. Which reminds us that most of our Christmas carols were written by people living in the Northern Hemisphere where it might snow on December 25. In fact, some people are dreaming of a white Christmas, I'm told. Maybe you're one of them!

**Exultant music**

Almost twenty years after Edward Caswell wrote the poetry for this carol, John Goss composed the music, and it is one of the most exultant carol tunes that we sing, especially the jubilant chorus ending each stanza, "Hail, thou ever-blessed morn!"

Organist at St. Paul's Cathedral, London, Goss was an earnest Christian musician, composer, and teacher of music; one of his pupils was Arthur Sullivan (of the famed comic opera duo Gilbert & Sullivan), and another was John Stainer. Stainer succeeded his teacher as organist at St. Paul's, and became a famous composer. Goss is also known for composing one of the grandest English hymn melodies; we sing it to Henry Lyte's "Praise My Soul the King of Heaven." Goss equally outdoes himself in the music to "See, Amid the Winter's Snow."

**Looking more closely**

The poet reminds us in the opening stanza that Jesus, the Lamb of God, was prophesied for centuries before the event. Much of Handel's oratorio "The Messiah" is based on these prophesies. From Genesis 3:15 and throughout the Old Testament, God makes promises. The incarnation of the Son of God at Christmas proves that God keeps his promises!

Each stanza ends with the chorus beginning, "Hail, thou ever blessed morn." Jesus' birth in Bethlehem (snowy or otherwise), was the morning, the "happy dawn" of redemption, the buying back of God's elect children by the Son. This is a message worth singing about, "Christ is born in Bethlehem."

The poet in the second stanza wants us to contemplate the vast contrast between "He who built the starry skies," Jesus as Creator God, but who is now lying in a manger as a helpless newborn baby; Jesus used to be "throned in height sublime," surrounded by angelic cherubim, but now, swaddled in a manger, he is hailed as the promised Messiah, the Christ now come to save his people from their sins.

In the third and fourth stanzas, the poet sets up a conversation; the shepherds are asked why they left their sheep uncared for out "On the lonely mountain steep?" What were they thinking? There's bears and lions out there! Careless with delight, the shepherds give their "joyful news" in their reply. "As we watched at dead of night/Lo, we saw a wondrous light." And they describe the angels, their message "of the Savior's birth," and that he had come to bring "Peace on earth."

The poet then shifts in the final two stanzas, directly addressing the "Sacred infant, all divine"; commending Jesus for his "tender love," and his leaving behind the "highest bliss" of heaven to come to earth, "to such a world as this." And then the persona speaking in the poetry resorts to praying. We only pray to God, Father, Son, and Holy Spirit. Any other kind of praying is idolatry. But Jesus, the "holy child," is who he says he is: the Son of God, the second person of the holy trinity, worthy of our supplication (our requests), adoration (our praises), and of our emulation. Emulation is when we want to be like Jesus, to resemble him, in his meekness—later Jesus would say that the meek are particularly blessed and will inherit the earth. We're to resemble him in being "mild," that is self-controlled, not given to violent reaction, throwing tantrums, and we're to be like him "in [his] sweet humility."

When Jesus saves us from our sins, he saves us to be like him, to love him, to obey him, to put off our sinful desires and behaviors, and to put on Jesus Christ. Christ's saving work is always accompanied by his sanctifying work; true saving faith will produce changes in us, most notably here in our walking with humility, like our Savior.

Sadly, the poet Caswell converted to Roman Catholicism just before writing this carol. He added another stanza that goes like this:

Virgin Mother, Mary blest
By the joys that fill thy breast,
Pray for us, that we may prove

Worthy of the Savior's love.
*Hail…*

**For discussion**

1. What is wrong with Caswell's last stanza, omitted in our hymnals? Is there a biblical and proper way in which we should appreciate and honor Mary for her role in the incarnation?
2. Read Mary's spontaneously composed carol in response to the angel visiting her in Luke 2:46-55.
3. Mary was likely only a young teenager when the angel announced to her that she was chosen by God to be Jesus' earthly mother. How do you think she was able to compose her *Magnificat*, such a beautiful and richly biblical carol?
4. Though we don't really know what season of the year in which Jesus was born, why do some of our carols like this one include winter and snow?
5. What does it mean to resemble Jesus? Do we do this just by working really hard? What is necessary for us to emulate him in his humility—and in any other of his qualities?

**On Christmas Night All Christians Sing**

Sussex Carol

Ralph Vaughan Williams (1872-1958)

(December 21)

On Christmas night all Christians sing
To hear the news the angels bring:
News of great joy, news of great mirth,
News of our merciful King's birth.

Then why should men on earth be sad,
Since our Redeemer made us glad,
When from our sin he set us free,
All for to gain our liberty?

When sin departs before his grace,
Then life and health come in its place;
Angels and men with joy may sing,
All for to see the newborn King.

All out of darkness we have light,
Which made the angels sing this night:

"Glory to God and peace to men,
Now and forevermore. Amen."

**Treasure hunting**

Imagine having a job where you go around the countryside, over hill, over dale, from tiny hamlet to medieval village searching for hidden treasure. That was what musician and composer Ralph Vaughan Williams spent as much time doing as he possibly could. And what treasure was he seeking? Folk tunes. Songs that had never been written down, never been sung in the concert hall or in the cathedral, but had been passed down orally, one generation singing and playing them to the next generation, over hundreds of years.

After serving in the Royal Army Medical Corps in World War I, Williams resumed his role as musician and composer, and took up a teaching post at the Royal College of Music in London.

He was a prolific composer, and he often adapted motifs from folk music melodies into his original compositions. Some of those compositions were written specifically for use in the singing of hymns by the congregation in Christian worship. So loved was he for his musical work, Williams was tasked with compiling and arranging hymn tunes for *The English Hymnal* published in 1906. In the Preface, he expressed his philosophy of church music: "Good music for worship is a moral issue.... The eternal gospel cannot be commended with disposable, fashionable music styles, otherwise there is the implication that the gospel itself is somehow disposable and temporary."

One day in 1904, while visiting a tiny hamlet called Monk's Gate, in the county of Sussex, England, Williams heard a local woman, Harriet Verrall singing a folk song he had never heard before—a Christmas song. Enchanted by the beauty of what he was hearing, he hastily wrote down the music. Though the poetry had first appeared in an obscure publication of Luke Wadding in 1682, "The Sussex Carol" tune had never before been heard beyond the confines of the country folks who lived in Sussex. After Williams discovered the beautiful folk tune, it rapidly charmed its way into wide-spread popularity—and into many hymnals.

**Looking more closely**

The angels' glad tidings to the shepherds were intended to be news of great joy for *all* types of people. Just as the Old Covenant temple was to be a house of prayer for all people, so the Good News the angels proclaimed was for all people without distinction of rank or importance. Why did God ordain that this glorious announcement would be brought to shepherds? Why not announced first to kings, princes, emperors?

We tend to think of shepherds in a very different light than they were esteemed in the Ancient Near Eastern world. Put bluntly, shepherds were considered untrustworthy rogues, only a tick above thugs; living out on the wilds with their sheep, they were smelly and considered ceremonially unclean by pious Jews. So little were they regarded by the civil society, a shepherd's testimony was not admissible in a court of law.

The opening line of the Sussex Carol reminds us that God's sovereign choice of those he would save from their sins was no respecter of persons. Jesus came to seek and to save that which was lost. The only precondition was being a needy sinner. Perhaps God intended to send the message to self-righteous Pharisees, that Jesus had come to save sinners—shepherds, the no-accounts, the misfits, the smoldering flax, the broken reed, the dregs of society—you and me! The angels' announcing the Messiah's birth to shepherds was a great offense to the religious elites. But it is "News of great joy, news of great mirth" for sinners like you and me. Our "merciful King's birth" for shepherds, for us, is Good News indeed!

In the second stanza, we're called to put away our sadness, "Since our Redeemer made us glad"! Unbelievers often think of Christians, true believers in Jesus, as people shackled to burdensome rules, dour folks, not having any fun. Shame on us if we send that message! We've been set free from our bondage to sin. Be glad! We've gained our liberty through our Redeemer Jesus! Be glad indeed!

The theme continues in the third stanza. Jesus' birth in Bethlehem was to pour out his grace, to make sin depart. The devil tells lies to you and to me. It's who he is. It's what he does. Sin is not fun, not in the end. He's a deceiver and tries hard to make sin look fun, but it's a lie. Being rid of our sins through Christ brings joy unspeakable. Seeing the "newborn King" makes "Angels and men with joy [to] sing"!

The final stanza reminds us that "All out of darkness we have light"; that's what the angels were so thrilled about and couldn't stop singing about that night when they roused the shepherds from their sleep with, "Glory to God and peace to men,/Now and forever, Amen"!

**For discussion**

1. Read Psalm 100:1-5 together. This was my father's favorite psalm; we recited it together with him moments before he went home to be with Jesus. What ought our response be to the Good News the angels proclaimed to the shepherds? How does Psalm 100:2 tell us we are to serve the Lord?
2. Have you noticed that some hymns, psalms, and carols are far easier to sing than others? Some words and the music they are set to make us *want* to join in. Can you see how Williams came to realize that folk tunes, music written for ordinary folks to sing, for average people, men and women, boys and girls—can you see why folk tunes made a lot of sense for the music we sing in church?
3. Discuss what Williams wrote about music for singing in church worship. "Good music for worship is a moral issue.... The eternal gospel cannot be commended with disposable, fashionable music styles, otherwise there is the implication that the gospel itself is somehow disposable and temporary." Do you agree or disagree, and why?
4. What ways does the devil tempt you to think that with sinning comes freedom and fun, and that walking in Jesus' will and way will make you unhappy?

5. Read Rev. 12:9 together. What are ways you can guard yourself against the lies and deceptions of the devil?

**Thou Didst Leave Thy Throne**

Emily E. S. Elliott (1836-1897)

(December 22)

Thou didst leave thy throne and thy kingly crown,
When thou camest to earth for me;
But in Bethlehem's home was there found no room
For thy holy nativity.
O come to my heart, Lord Jesus,
There is room in my heart for thee.

Heaven's arches rang when the angels sang,
Proclaiming thy royal degree;
But of lowly birth didst thou come to earth,
And in great humility.
O come to my heart, Lord Jesus,
There is room in my heart for thee.

The foxes found rest, and the birds their nest
In the shade of the forest tree;
But thy couch was the sod, O thou Son of God,

In the deserts of Galilee.
O come to my heart, Lord Jesus,
There is room in my heart for thee.

Thou camest, O Lord, with the living word
That should set thy people free;
But with mocking scorn, and with crown of thorn,
They bore thee to Calvary.
O come to my heart, Lord Jesus,
There is room in my heart for thee.

When the heavens shall ring, and the angels sing,
At thy coming to victory,
Let thy voice call me home, saying "Yet there is room,
There is room at my side for thee."
My heart shall rejoice, Lord Jesus,
When thou comest and callest for me.

**My mother and this carol**

My mother tells the story of when my generous father gave our family home away to support Christian education—lock, stock, and barrel. That was my father. Tears streaming down her cheeks, my mother did one final walk through the home in which they had raised me. When she caught a glimpse of her tear-stained face in the vanity mirror, the opening stanza of Emily Elliott's carol suddenly sprang to mind. "Thou didst leave thy throne and they kingly crown/When thou camest to earth for me..." My godly mother was struck by how much more Jesus left behind when he came to earth to become our Savior—and here she was weeping about leaving our family home behind? Bolstered by the words of this carol, she dried her eyes and gratefully said her goodbyes to the old house.

### About the poet

The poet who penned this carol, Emily Elliott, was the daughter of an Anglican minister, the pastor of St. Marks, Brighton, on the south coast of England. She grew up with a deep love and concern for the sick and the poor in her day. Her aunt was Charlotte Elliott, the hymn writer who wrote "Just as I am," the often-repeated lyric sung many times over at revival meetings. In my youth, I once counted; I'm pretty sure we sang it twenty-one times in a single meeting!

The Elliott family's historical moment was a time of social reform. The Industrial Revolution had left many people to be treated as mere cogs in the machine of industry; child labor was rampant, and abuse of workers was evident in almost every factory and family.

Correspondingly, it was a time of philanthropy, a love of humanity, when many Christians developed a deep concern for the poor and downtrodden, as Elliott did. All of these things are good; the true believer will love his neighbor, especially his poor and oppressed neighbor.

But there's the ever-present danger of reducing the gospel of Jesus Christ into a temporal message of making the world a better place from which to go to hell. Sadly, many nominal Christians and liberals reduced the gospel to social reform in Elliott's day—and many progressives do so today. Christian socialism reduces Jesus' incarnation into him being merely the supreme example of how to care for the poor and needy in this life—but they have no room in their hearts for a Jesus who is the Son of God and the only Savior of sinners from eternal death in hell. They didn't have any place for that overly zealous evangelism stuff!

It's no mere coincidence that Karl Marx book on communism and socialism *Das Kapital* was published in 1859, smack-dab in the middle of these social reform movements spreading across England (Marx died in London, his body buried in Highgate Cemetery, not far from Christina Rossetti's). And it's no surprise that *Origin of Species* by Englishman Charles Darwin was published the same year; the secularization of society's beliefs had many allies. Charles Dickens wrote his famous *A Christmas Carol* in the same historical timeframe and milieu, hence his caricature of Scrooge as the money-grubbing skinflint, miserly Capitalist, bilking the poor. Elliott penned this carol in 1864, encircled by these same social reforming movements.

There were real abuses in mid-19th century England that needed to be corrected. But the best men knew that the gospel was the ultimate solution, because only the gospel of Jesus Christ changes the heart. "Other men may teach socialism," declared C. H. Spurgeon, who ministered in England at this same time, "deliver lectures, or collect a band of fiddlers that they may gather a congregation, but I will preach the gospel." Compassionate toward the poor as he was, Spurgeon understood the danger of diluting the gospel into a social reform project—and thereby reducing Jesus into simply a champion of income equality. We're very much in danger of repeating the same errors today. It shouldn't have to be either or.

We need the incarnation of Jesus to save us from our sins, and Christians need to love their poor neighbors and help them with both hands: the gospel for their souls' sake—first and last—and then help them learn to earn money for their food and clothing, and to do whatever we can to help alleviate their hunger and to keep them warm in the process.

**Looking more closely**

Do you notice the contrast Elliott creates in each stanza? The first two lines of the first two stanzas are about the difference between what Jesus left behind in heaven, his "throne" and "kingly crown," and the humble circumstances of his life on earth, "in Bethlehem's home was there found no room." Jesus was the central feature of heaven, flanked and hailed by angel hosts proclaiming his royal status; there was ample room for him in heaven! "But of lowly birth didst thou come to earth/And in great humility." There wasn't even a proper room for Mary to give birth to Jesus here on earth. Do you see the vast contrast? Then each stanza ends with a prayer of consecration and invitation, "O come to my heart, Lord Jesus/There is room in my heart for thee."

In Matthew 8:20, Jesus says that foxes and birds have places to lay down their heads at night and sleep, but in the third stanza we learn that Jesus had nowhere to lay his head "In the deserts of Galilee." Here, we see more contrast between what Jesus left in the glories of heaven for his humiliation and incarnation here on earth.

In the fourth stanza, we learn that Jesus' Word is what sets us free from our sin, but it would come at a great price, "with mocking scorn, and with crown of thorn." And then Jesus would be led away to be crucified at Calvary for our salvation.

In the final stanza, Elliott gives us a peek at the Second Advent, when Jesus will come again, this time in victory, and he will call us home to be with him in heaven. Jesus has made a room for us, and at his side for evermore. What is our response to such a Savior? "My heart shall rejoice, Lord Jesus"! Is there room in your heart for the Lord Jesus?

**For discussion**

1. Did Jesus stop being the sovereign King of kings when he was born in Bethlehem? Compare Elliott's opening stanza with these lines from Charles Wesley's other carol:

   Born thy people to deliver,
   Born a child and yet a King,
   Born to reign in us forever,
   Now thy gracious kingdom bring.

1. Read and discuss Philippians 2:3-11. Compare what Paul says about what Jesus laid aside in the incarnation with this carol.
2. According to Luke 2:7, there was no room for Mary and Joseph in the inn. Throughout his earthly ministry, Jesus was despised and rejected by many. How about you? Is there room in your heart for Jesus, your whole heart?

3. Jesus won't just live in one little chamber, maybe the guest room or the garage; Jesus came to fill and transform your entire being. Discuss together as family what that should look like in your home, in your life.
4. Elliott wrote this carol for the children in her father's congregation in Brighton, and to be sung by the church choir for Advent. Do you see features that indicate it was intentionally composed for children?
5. Elliott wrote this carol in the midst of what is called Revivalism; the evangelism of the day was significantly influenced by Arminian theology, a theology that places emphasis on man's free will as causative in salvation; it often reduces the message of salvation into a call to invite Jesus into your heart. Do you see elements of this in her carol? Does the Bible ever tell you to invite Jesus into your heart?

**Lo, How a Rose E'er Blooming**

German hymn, circa 16th century
Michael Praetorius (1571-1621)
(December 23)

Lo, how a rose e'er blooming
From tender stem hath sprung!
Of Jesse's lineage coming
As prophets long have sung,
It came, a floweret bright,
Amid the cold of winter,
When half-spent was the night.

Isaiah 'twas foretold it,
The rose I have in mind;
With Mary we behold it,
The virgin mother kind.
To show God's love aright,
She bore to us a Savior,
When half-spent was the night.

This flower, whose fragrance tender
With sweetness fills the air,

Dispels with glorious splendor
The darkness everywhere.
True man, yet very God,
From sin and death he saves us
And lightens every load.

O Savior, child of Mary,
Who felt our human woe;
O Savior, King of glory,
Who dost our weakness know:
Bring us at length we pray
To the bright courts of heaven,
And to the endless day.

**A German Christmas carol**

We know that "Lo, How a Rose E'er Blooming" was written by a German poet in the same century as Martin Luther and the Protestant Reformation. Because it was penned in German, it was almost certainly written by a Protestant, since Rome forbade the singing of psalms and hymns in the vernacular, the language ordinary people spoke. We know that Lutheran poet and musician Michael Praetorius had a significant hand in composing or arranging the music. He was a prolific poet and composer, credited with over a thousand pieces of church music, and so it is highly possible that he wrote the poetry as well.

Praetorius was one of those people who died on his birthday (born February 15, 1571; died February 15, 1621), which throughout his life, on his birthday, he never knew it would also be his death day. Which gives us the opportunity to pause and reflect; as the days pass on the calendar, each one of us is passing over the month and day on which we will breathe our last breath and die. Far from a morbid reflection, this consideration ought to help us do what the psalmist tells us to do, "number our days aright" (Psalm 90:12), and thereby gain a heart of wisdom.

**Looking more closely**

Have you noticed in your Bible reading how often God wants us to look at the flowers? "Consider the lilies" (Matthew 6:28), we're encouraged to do. God made such an amazing variety of beautiful flowers—there's a great deal to consider about them! In Song of Solomon 2:1 we read, "I am a rose of Sharon..." And in Isaiah 35:1-2 we read about the wilderness profusely blossoming, with the majesty of Sharon, a plain in ancient Israel that was noted for its beautiful flowers.

The symbolism is not as clear as biblical scholars would like, but many believe the rose of Sharon was a metaphor for Christ, others insist it is referring to Mary (hence, Roman Catholics pray the rosary). What is clear is that when Jesus comes the second time, he will make the wilderness and the desert places to sprout and bloom profusely with lovely flowers, roses, crocuses, tulips! When Jesus restores all things in this thorn-infested, sin-sick world, it will overwhelm us with its beauty. Imagine the floral scents and sights of the Garden of Eden before the Fall. When the desert blossoms, it will be even more lovely and perfect—and no more possibility of sin corrupting and making the flowers wither and fall off. Won't that be glorious!

"Of Jesse's lineage coming," refers to Isaiah's prophecy that Jesus will spring from the Davidic line, Jesse being King David's father, "As prophets long have sung." Notice in the second stanza, the German poet makes an appearance in his own poetry, "The rose I have in mind," and he invites us to behold all this through Mary's eyes, who "bore to us a Savior."

In the third stanza, after more floral imagery, the poet shifts from the half-spent night of Jesus birth to him dispelling "with glorious splendor/The darkness everywhere." The German Lutheran poet next alludes to lines from the Nicaean Creed (AD 325) where both Jesus' deity and humanity are asserted, here in the carol with the words, "True man, yet very God." And why was Jesus born to the virgin Mary?

Why the incarnation of the Son of God? "From sin and death he saves us/And lightens every load." Jesus himself told us his yoke was easy and his burden light (Matthew 11:30). Just as John Bunyan (1678) portrays the pilgrim weighed down and crushed by the burden of his sins, Jesus came to lighten every load, to bear our sins in his own body on the cross. Our burden is lifted! Rejoice! Jesus came to bear all on our behalf, "To show God's love aright."

The final stanza reminds us that our Savior in his humanity "felt our human woe" and knew our every weakness. However dark the trouble that enters your life, Jesus knows and felt, and has carried the burden of that trouble intimately. And as our "Savior, King of glory," he will bring us "To the bright courts of heaven" where there will be no more darkness—only "endless day[s]" of rejoicing and worshiping, feasting and praising the "Savior, child of Mary." And, my guess, is there will be a vast array of beautiful flowers in heaven!

**For discussion**

1. What was unusual about when Michael Praetorius was born and when he died? You know your birthday. But since you do not know on what day you will die, how should you live each day God gives you on this earth?
2. In the opening line in the original German of this carol the German word is not "rose" but *reis,* which means "twig" or "branch." Does that change the meaning, and, if so, how?
3. Read Isaiah 4:2 and compare with Jeremiah 23:5. Who is the branch (or twig) about whom the prophets are foretelling?
4. Read and discuss I Peter 1:24-25. Your father likely buys roses for your mother on special occasions. You've noticed what happens to those lovely roses after a few days, maybe a week; the flowers wither, and the petals fall off. Of what does this reality remind us about our lives?

**O Little Town of Bethlehem**

Phillips Brooks (1835-1893)

(December 24)

O little town of Bethlehem,
How still we see thee lie;
Above thy deep and dreamless sleep
The silent stars go by:
Yet in thy dark streets shineth
The everlasting Light;
The hopes and fears of all the years
Are met in thee tonight.

For Christ is born of Mary;
And gathered all above,
While mortals sleep, the angels keep
Their watch of wondering love.
O morning stars, together

Proclaim the holy birth!
And praises sing to God the King,
And peace to men on earth.

How silently, how silently,
The wondrous gift is given!
So God imparts to human hearts
The blessings of his heaven.
No ear may hear his coming,
But in this world of sin,
Where meek souls will receive him still,
The dear Christ enters in.

O holy Child of Bethlehem,
Descend to us, we pray;
Cast out our sin and enter in;
Be born in us today.
We hear the Christmas angels
The great glad tidings tell;
O come to us, abide with us,
Our Lord Emmanuel.

**About the poet**

Standing six-feet-eight-inches tall, Pastor Phillips Brooks, minister at Holy Trinity in Philadelphia, was a giant of a man. He was known particularly as an evangelist, and as a friend of children. Though he never married and so had no offspring of his own, he was much loved by the children in his flock. He kept toys in his church office, and reportedly it was not uncommon to see the big parson on his knees on the floor playing with the children.

In 1865, Brooks went on a trip to Jerusalem in December. On Christmas Eve, he rode on horseback from Jerusalem to Bethlehem, passing the hillside on which it is said the angel hosts announced the birth of Christ to the shepherds. That evening, he attended a candlelight service at the Church of the Holy Nativity, believed by some to have been built over the place where Jesus was born. Pastor Brooks was much moved by that experience.

Three years later, only days before Christmas, while reminiscing about his visit to Bethlehem, he felt the desire to write a Christmas carol for the children in his parish. "I remember especially on Christmas Eve," he wrote, "when I was standing in the old church in Bethlehem, close to the spot where Jesus was born, when the whole church was ringing hour after hour with the splendid hymns of praise to God, how again and again it seemed as if I could hear voices I knew well, telling each other of the wonderful night of the Savior's birth."

Sharpening his quill, Brooks sat down at his desk and wrote, "O Little Town of Bethlehem." Christmas was just around the corner, but he had no tune to go with his new carol. He showed the poem to his organist, Lewis Redner and asked him if he could compose a suitable tune.

Redner described what happened next: "As Christmas of 1868 approached, Mr. Brooks told me that he had written a simple little carol for the Christmas Sunday-school service, and he asked me to write the tune to it." But, try as he did, the organist was stumped. He couldn't think of any music to go with his pastor's carol. On Friday, Brooks checked in with his organist about the music. Distressed, Redner had to tell him there *was* no music, not yet, but he would try to have the tune in time for the Sunday Christmas service—less than forty-eight hours away. "On the Saturday night," wrote Redner, "my brain was all confused about the tune... But I was roused from sleep late in the night hearing an angel-strain whispering in my ear, and seizing a piece of music paper I jotted down the treble of the tune as we now have it, and on Sunday morning before going to church I filled in the harmony."

How could a carol written at the eleventh hour of a Christmas Eve become such a favorite, especially among children? "The simple music was written in great haste and under great pressure," wrote Redner. "Neither Mr. Brooks nor I ever thought the carol or the music to it would live beyond that Christmas of 1868." Yet here it is more than 150 years later.

Brooks died suddenly and unexpectedly at fifty-eight years old; his congregation deeply grieved at his loss. When one mother told her daughter that their beloved pastor had died, the little girl exclaimed, "Oh Mama, how happy the angels will be."

### Looking more closely

In the opening line of the first stanza, Brooks chose to personify and directly address the town of Bethlehem. He evokes in us the sense of a quiet little place, wholly unaware of the stupendous visitation about to illuminate the dark streets of the village. Unassuming place that it was, "The everlasting Light" was being born there. Don't despise the day of small things: "The hopes and fears of all the years/Are met in thee tonight." God had promised that he would send his Son. This was the night. The promise is fulfilled. Jesus had come at last.

The second stanza reminds us that "Christ is born of Mary," and "While mortals sleep," everybody in Bethlehem, except Mary and Joseph, were likely sound asleep, but not the angel hosts; they stood watch with "wondering love." Though the star that would later lead the wisemen to Bethlehem did not appear the night Jesus was born, Brooks chose to hint at that star by including the "morning stars," along with the angels, "Proclaim[ing] the holy birth!" The poet alludes to what the angels sang "to God the King," of "peace to men on earth."

Then in the third stanza, Brooks emphasizes the silence of that unassuming town, "how still we see thee lie," and the "silent stars go by." The poet wants us to feel the contrast between the cosmic events afoot with the silence and stillness; imagine the King of kings born in the unpretentious, quiet, little town of Bethlehem. We're reminded of Joseph Mohr's carol, "Silent Night," in which he too emphasized the silence, as if the whole world were holding its breath in astonishment at the great events taking place in the little town.

God often comes as a "still, small voice," not with the pomp and bombast we expect at the birth of a great king. "The wondrous gift is given" not with great fanfare, in triumphal parade, in courtly palace, but in an unimportant little town, likely in a stable, where the infant King was laid not in a gold-gilded cradle, but in a feeding trough for cattle.

Brooks then reminds us of the truth of sovereign grace that "God imparts to human hearts/The blessing of his heaven." Salvation is not a co-equal partnership where God does his part and we do our part; God is the acting subject doing the imparting—*all* the imparting. "In this world of sin," all we contribute to our salvation is our sin. God makes our hearts receptive, "meek souls," and convicts us of our great sin and our need of a great Savior. To those souls, and those alone, "The dear Christ enters in."

Ever the evangelist, in the final stanza Brooks resorts to prayer, "O holy Child of Bethlehem." He's no longer speaking to the town, as in the first stanza, but directly to the infant King. He calls on Jesus to "Descend to us," and alludes to what Jesus later told Nicodemus, "You must be born again" (John 3:7). Jesus alone could "Cast out our sin and enter in/Be born in us today." Jesus is Emmanuel, God with us, and here he is! Can you pray with the poet, "O come to us, abide with us/Our Lord Emmanuel"?

**For discussion**

1. Read together Micah 5:2. What does it tell us about Bethlehem? How did Brooks weave the description in this verse into the carol?
2. Read John 3:1-21. What was Nicodemus so confused about? Everybody alive has been born once. How do you get born again? What does that mean? Have you been born again?

3. Though this carol was written for children, what are some examples of the deep theological doctrines imbedded in the poetry?
4. Discuss why Brooks and Mohr (and others) emphasized silence at the coming and birth of Jesus? Read Job 21:5 and 40:4. When God comes down and answers Job, what does Job do? When we are tempted to complain, what should we do?

## Who is This, So Weak and Helpless

William Walsham How (1823-1897)

(December 25)

Who is this, so weak and helpless,
Child of lowly Hebrew maid,
Rudely in a stable sheltered,
Coldly in a manger laid?
'Tis the Lord of all creation,
Who this wondrous path has trod;
He is God from everlasting,
And to everlasting God.

Who is this, a Man of Sorrows,
Walking sadly life's hard way,
Homeless, weary, sighing, weeping
Over sin and Satan's sway?
'Tis our God, our glorious Savior,
Who above the starry sky

Is for us a place preparing,
Where no tear can dim the eye.

Who is this? Behold him shedding
Drops of blood upon the ground!
Who is this, despised, rejected,
Mocked, insulted, beaten, bound?
'Tis our God, who gifts and graces
On his church is pouring down;
Who shall smite in holy vengeance
All his foes beneath his throne.

Who is this that hangs there dying
While the rude world scoffs and scorns,
Numbered with the malefactors,
Torn with nails, and crowned with thorns?
'Tis our God, who lives forever
'Mid the shining ones on high,
In the glorious golden city,
Reigning everlastingly.

**About the poet**

Most of my heroes from church history were not fond of bishops, Catholic *or* Anglican ones. The best Reformers considered bishops a hold-over from the manifold errors of Rome; like the papacy, the office of bishop was not an office found in a biblical doctrine of the church by the best men of the Reformation: Calvin, Knox, Luther, to name a few. The Puritans, more of my heroes, got their name from wanting to purify the Anglican church from its papal impurities, including getting rid of bishops. But we must not dismiss all bishops as money-grubbing, time-serving, pompous charlatans. Many of them were, especially in Scotland, but there were several notable exceptions.

Anglican pastor William Walsham How earned the reputation as "The poor-man's bishop," and "The people's bishop." Unlike many grasping Anglican churchmen, using the church as their means of advancement in society and culture, Bishop How was a Christ-like, sacrificial servant who genuinely cared for the souls of his flock. He aspired to be the sort of pastor the common man would want to be at his side on his deathbed, a man full of gospel grace, gentleness, and love.

After declining the Bishopric of Durham, one of the most coveted appointments for a cleric in his day, How served at humble Abby Church near the Welsh border, an ancient building, nearly a thousand years old, in a parish made up of working-class people, many of them Welsh, some with faces blackened with coal from the mines. A notable feature of the Welsh—they loved singing hymns—and not just in church.

Perhaps as an extension of his desire to nurture and edify his flock, and influenced by the Welsh love of hymn singing, How set his quill to paper and wrote a number of hymns, several in continuous use since his death. "For all the Saints," is one of his finest hymns.

In 1896, the year before his death, Bishop How was asked what makes a poem a good hymn. It's a form of the question we've been exploring in these Advent devotions: what makes a carol a good carol? He replied, "A good hymn is something like a good prayer—simple, real, earnest, and reverent."

Pastor How's "Who is This, So Weak and Helpless" carol was set to the tune *Eifionydd* composed by Welshman John Ambrose Lloyd. Welsh tunes are some of the most singable melodies in church history. After all, they were composed as folk tunes, intended to be sung with gusto by everybody: miners and merchants, mothers and maidens, boys and bishops; men, women, and children of ever station in life—which is what Christ's church is made of. They were tunes "For all the saints."

Bishop How's carol is a poem that cannot be subsumed by popular musical sounds. His grand lyric demands a substantial, appropriate, and worthy tune to sustain the stupendous weight of the theme—Jesus' birth, sinless life, betrayal, him being forsaken by his Father, his crucifixion, and his final and future glorious triumph; judgment enacted and eternity won. There is no happy-clappy pop tune capable of undergirding such grandeur. The robust tune *Eifionydd*, on the other hand, has the musical muscle to bear the weight of this marvelous carol.

**Looking more closely**

Do you remember William Chatterton Dix's carol "What Child is This?" Both of these carols use the poetic device of asking a question, prompting curiosity in the reader, singer, worshiper. In the opening quatrain (four lines) of the first stanza, Bishop How demonstrates the humiliation of our Lord by using a series of evocative descriptive words like "weak," "helpless," "lowly," "rudely," and "coldly." Who is this baby born of an insignificant Hebrew unmarried woman, sheltered in a stable, and laid in a manger? It is a compelling question. On its face, we may be inclined to assume someone so low born must be a nobody, obscure, entirely insignificant. Unbelievers persist in this conclusion to this day—to their everlasting peril.

The second quatrain of each stanza answers the question from the first quatrain. *Gloriously* answers the questions! Pastor How thrills our hearts with his answer. The seemingly insignificant "weak and helpless" infant born to such humble, abject ignominy "is the Lord of all creation"! Make no mistake. The infant who lies there in that cold, rude, lowly manger bed—is the everlasting God who made all things!

Though it begins at Jesus' birth, this carol is not included in the Advent-themed portion of many hymnals because the majority of the hymn is about Jesus' earthly ministry, his passion, and suffering on the cross, and his Second Advent. The second stanza leaves behind his lowly birth and poses the next question, "Who is this, a Man of Sorrows," and then continues with another string of evocative descriptors such as "sadly," "hard," "Homeless, weary, sighing, weeping." Life was a vale of tears for our Lord, and it often is for his faithful people. But then in the second quatrain of the stanza, the poet thrills us once again with his answer: "'Tis our God, our glorious Savior," who is preparing for us a place in heaven "Where no tear can dim the eye."

In the third stanza, How turns his lens to Gethsemane, Jesus so anguished in prayer before his Father that he was "shedding/Drops of blood upon the ground." And then our Lord was "despised, rejected/Mocked, insulted, beaten, bound." This is no overstatement of the brutality of Christ's misery. The poet masterfully marshals this barrage of verbs to awaken in us the incalculable suffering our Lord underwent on our behalf. Who would undergo such torment?

"Who is this?" The poet gives answer. "'Tis our God," who pours out on his church, his bride, his people, "gifts and graces." Still more, there is a day coming when our God "shall smite in holy vengeance/All his foes beneath his throne." Our holy God of justice is not mocked. Never forget the sobering reflection: When we say in the Lord's Prayer, "Thy kingdom come," we are praying for Jesus to return in triumph and rain down his judgment and wrath upon all his and our enemies.

In the last question in the final stanza, "Who is this that hangs there dying?" the poet reminds us of the first stanza using a form of the same word as bookends; it's called a poetic inclusio, accomplished here with the word "rude." The one who was laid "rudely" in a stable as an infant, now faces the "rude world," that "scoffs and scorns" (in poetry, words near each other that begin with the same consonant letter are called an alliteration). We can almost hear the crack of the scourging whip, the taunting mockery, in the double alliteration, "scoffs and scorns."

The perfectly holy Son of God is "numbered with the malefactors," crucified with thieves and murderers; "Torn with nails, and crowned with thorns." Who is this man? "'Tis our God, who lives forever." As a man, Jesus submitted himself to the most heinous execution imaginable, and he died. But How wants us to feel the full weight of the cosmic irony. Jesus the Son of God who died a brutal death on that Roman gibbet, "lives forever"! The grave could not keep him. He arose, he was seen of men, he ascended "on high/In the glorious golden city," where he rules and reigns everlastingly.

Today is Christmas! As you celebrate, open gifts, feast, sing, laugh together as a family, bear in mind why we are celebrating. Ask yourselves the question, "Who is this…?" "What Child is this?" And then join your merry voices together in worship with the answer: "'Tis our God, who lives forever."

## For discussion

1. When did you last cry? Why do you think God made us so that we shed tears about some things? The poet ends the second stanza with "Where no tear can dim the eye." Read Psalm 56:8 and compare with Revelation 21:4.
2. The carol, "Away in a Manger," includes the phrase, "no crying he makes." Jesus was fully God but also fully man (yet without sin). Do you think Jesus cried as an infant? Read the shortest verse in the Bible, John 11:35. Did Jesus ever shed tears?
3. What word does the poet use as bookends, as an inclusio in the carol? We use that same word somewhat differently today; you might say that your brother is being this. Discuss what the word means in How's poetry.
4. Christ's First Advent is called his humiliation. The Westminster Shorter Catechism put it like

this: Q. 27: Wherein did Christ's humiliation consist? A: "Christ's humiliation consisted in his being born, and that in a low condition, made under the law, undergoing the miseries of this life, the wrath of God, and the cursed death of the cross; in being buried, and continuing under the power of death for a time." Discuss phrases from How's carol hymn that correspond with Jesus' humiliation?

5. How well do you think the poet measured up in this carol to his own description of what makes a good hymn? "A hymn is essentially a form of devotion. It is a channel through which the soul's best and highest emotions and aspirations should flow. A good hymn is something like a good prayer—simple, real, earnest, and reverent. Of course, it demands some chastened beauty of expression, and sensitive choice of language. The charm and the power of a good hymn depend upon subtle and delicate qualities, which are more easily felt than analyzed. Perhaps purity of tone, admitting no shade of affectation or exaggeration on the one side, or of stiffness or uncomeliness on the other, would describe the first necessary attribute of a really good hymn" (William Walsham How, "Hymns," *Werner's Magazine*, vol. 18, no. 8 (August 1896), 756).

MERRY CHRISTMAS!

Douglas Bond, father of six, and grandfather of ten and counting, is a hymn writer, an award-winning teacher, award-winning script writer, and author of more than thirty-five books of historical fiction, biography, and practical theology, several translated into Dutch, Portuguese, Romanian, and Korean. He speaks internationally at churches, schools, and conferences, directs the Oxford Creative Writing Master Class, and leads Church history and hymn tours. Find out more and listen to musical renditions of these carols at bondbooks.net/hymns.

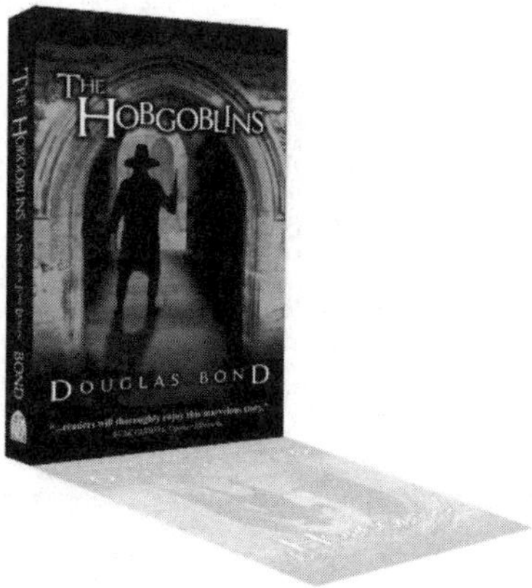


"A super, gripping story based around the bet-selling author of all time – John Bunyan. I don't think I have read a book so quickly in my life! I thought I was reasonably well-versed in John Bunyan but, putting it into historical context brings it all to life, and I have learned."
**— John Hinson, Minister, Elstow Abbey and Abbey tour guide**

"Even readers who've not read John Bunyan's Pilgrim's Progress will thoroughly enjoy this marvelous story."
**— Burk Parsons, senior pastor, St Andrew's Chapel; chief publishing officer, Ligonier Ministries; editor, *Tabletalk Magazine***

"In this exciting and moving book, Douglas Bond introduces readers to one of Christianity's great heroes. Written from the perspective of Bunyan's rogue friend turned jailer, this lively story echoes with Bunyan's own words as he passed through many trials and temptations on his pilgrim way to the Celestial City."
**— Dr. Joel Beeke, President, Puritan Reformed Theological Seminary, Grand Rapids, Michigan**

"John Bunyan's 'Christian' lived a remarkable, grace-filled life of adventure. Christian's creator John Bunyan lived a similarly remarkable, grace-filled life of adventure, too. You already know Christian. Now get ready to read this cleverly crafted book by Douglas Bond to get to know his creator."
**— Stephen P. Nichols, President, Reformation Bible College and Ligonier Ministries**

"*God Sings!* is an engaging book that helps attune our hearts and minds to hear the voice of God in Scripture."

**JULIA CAMERON**, author, Oxford publicist, and Fellow of the Royal Society of Arts

"In ***God Sings!***, Douglas Bond provides us with a sure, biblically faithful, and robustly theological guide to thoughtful, God-centered, Christ-exalting, gospel-magnifying praise. In an evangelical world increasingly noted more for triviality than substance, *God Sings!* is a clarion call to the Church to give God the praise of which he alone is worthy."

**DR. IAN HAMILTON** teaches at Greenville Presbyterian Theological Seminary; and at Westminster PTS, Newcastle, England; and is a Trustee of the Banner of Truth Trust, Edinburgh, Scotland

"Anyone familiar with Douglas Bond's other works will know him as a great storyteller. ***Grace Works*** is about the greatest story of all: the gospel. Issuing from the faith of a recipient of God's Good News and the care of a shepherd, any wounds inflicted here will be those of a friend. Grace is not the enemy of works but the only proper source. It's amazing how many ways we can get that wrong—usually, as Doug argues, by incremental and often imperceptible changes. There is a lot of wisdom in this book, but none greater than the wisdom that Christ is and gives us in his gospel."

**MICHAEL HORTON**, J. Gresham Machen Professor of Systematic Theology and Apologetics

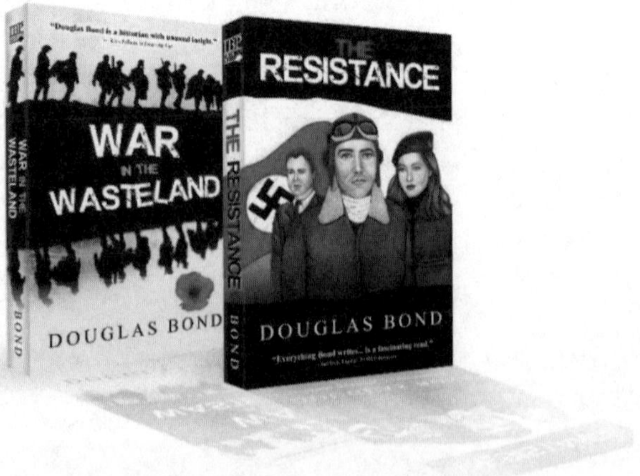


"*War in the Wasteland* is proof positive of what I have known for many years now: Douglas Bond is a great storyteller. Indeed, this novel combines all the attributes of a can't-put-it-down thriller with the intellectual tensions of a historical drama: taut plotting, strong characters, and soaring backdrop. Put this one on the top of your must-read list."

**GEORGE GRANT**, author, teacher, pastor at Parish Presbyterian Church

"If you enjoy inspirational war stories, flying, intrigue, mystery, and intense anticipation, you will love Douglas Bond's new book ***The Resistance***. Not only is the action non-stop, but the thoughtful dialogue throughout the tale keeps you mentally engaged on every page."

**DOUGLAS E. LEE**, Brigadier General, USA (Ret), President, Chaplain Alliance for Religious Liberty

"***Luther in Love***, a fitting tribute to one of the most fascinating power-couples of the ages! With the skill of a scholar and the sparkle of a bard, Douglas Bond weaves together a thrilling and engaging story."

**ERIC LANDRY**, Executive Editor, *Modern Reformation*

"If you enjoy reading the fictional works of C. S. Lewis, you will love ***The Betrayal***."

**BURK PARSONS**, editor, *Tabletalk*

"In ***The Thunder***, Douglas Bond deftly escorts us into the 16th century world of John Knox. Bond's careful use of language…the seamless flow, rich, vivid picture of Scotland and Reformation. The spiritual aspect of the story richer... A fine work."

**LIZ CURTIS HIGGS**, best-selling author of the Lowlands of Scotland series

"In ***The Revolt***, Douglas Bond uses his unique writing style to produce a highly readable imagining of the travails of John Wycliffe, ...a vivid and exciting narrative..."

**BOB CRESON**, President/CEO, Wycliffe Bible Translators, USA

Neil Perkins, a student at Haltwhistle Grammar School in England, unearths an ancient Roman manuscript. After dedicating himself to studying Latin, he uncovers a story of treachery and betrayal from the 3rd century.

"Enjoyable reading for anyone who likes a gripping, fast-paced Adventure story, ***Hostage Lands*** will especially delight young students of Latin and Roman history."

**STARR MEADE**, author of *Grandpa's Box*

Half-Saxon, half-Dane, misfit Cynwulf lives apart from the world in a salvaged Viking ship, dreaming of spending his life with the fair Haeddi. When he is accused of murder, he must clear his name before he loses everything to the vengeance of the community that has already rejected him.

"In ***Hand of Vengeance*** Douglas Bond shines a light on the past in a way that's as entertaining as it is informative."

**JANIE B. CHEANEY**, senior writer, WORLD magazine

## CROWN & COVENANT TRILOGY

The Crown & Covenant trilogy follows the lives of the M'Kethe family as they endure persecution in 17th century Scotland and later flee to colonial America. Douglas Bond weaves together fictional characters and historical figures from Scottish Covenanting history.

"Will lift you into the 17th century and onto the moorlands of Scotland. This is the danger-zone, inhabited by evil, death, courage, and faith. A story not to be missed."

**SINCLAIR FERGUSON**, Chancellor's Professor of Systematic Theology at RTS

"Douglas Bond has introduced a new generation to the heroics of the Scottish Covenanters, and he has done it in a delightful way."

**LIGON DUNCAN**, Chancellor/CEO of Reformed Theological Seminary and the John E. Richards Professor of Systematic and Historical Theology